AF559723

Critical Response to Indian Fiction in English

Edited by
AMAR NATH PRASAD

ATLANTIC PUBLISHERS AND DISTRIBUTORS

Published by
ATLANTIC PUBLISHERS AND DISTRIBUTORS
B-2, Vishal Enclave, New Delhi-110 027
Phones : 541 3460, 542 9987

Sales Office
4215/1, Ansari Road, Darya Ganj, New Delhi-110 002
Phones : 327 3880, 328 5873, 328 0451
Fax : 91-11-328 5873
e-mail : info@atlanticbooks.com
web : www.atlanticbooks.com

ISBN 81-7156-947-1

Typeset at
APD Computer Graphics, Delhi

Printed in India at
Nice Printing Press, Delhi

PREFACE

After the marathan efforts of Raja Ram Mohan Roy, English language came into existence in 1935 and since then a new intellectual and literary vista opened before the people of India which awakened their literary and creative genius. It was during the later half of the 19th century, when English literature in India began to take its root and shoot. But the real flowering came in the form of fictions by a number of good and great novelists like K.S. Venkataramani, Mulk Raj Anand, R.K. Narayan, Raja Rao, Bhabani Bhattacharya, Kamala Markandaya, Anita Desai and many more. In modern fictions, Vikram Seth's *A Suitable Boy*, Arundhati Roy's *The God of Small Things*, Mahasweta Devi's *The Mother of 1084* and Manju Kapur's *Difficult Daughters* have shot into international limelight by winning prestigious awards of global acclaim. These writers, specially the women novelists, have created and are creating such a vision of life both thematically and aesthetically that now it is wrong to say that great art can be rendered only in the artist's mother tongue. Today we see that the authors of the creative Indian fiction have managed to overcome this insurmountable hurdle. The present trend of Indo-Anglian fictions obviously shows a bright and optimistic future — such a future which is bound to yield fruits and flowers provided the plant is properly irrigated, nourished and pruned.

The present volume is a humble attempt to present a critical view of the fictions in Indo-Anglian literature. I have tried my best to select only those articles which dive deep into the hidden depth of Indian Fictions in English and churn out generative and constructive criticism of the work concerned. The leading article, "Gandhian Impact on Indo-Anglian Fictions," concisely presents the works of those Indian novelists who are richly enamoured by the ideals of M.K. Gandhi. It also shows how the novelists, in spite of their truthful portrayal of the society, particularly of Gandhism, never deviate from aesthetic touch or metaphorical exactitude, the heart of any great work of art.

In his article, "The Reflection of Socio-Political Changes in the Indian English," Prof. S.N. Jha focuses the attention on the turbulent undercurrent of East-West encounter culminating abundantly in socio-political changes in the fictions written before and after Independence. He opines that despite many hurdles, Indian English fiction has treaded a long way and is presently flourishing without any full stop.

Dr. N.D.R. Chandra analytically examines the piteous plight of women proliferated through various identities — national, ethnic, sexual, gender and so on. He is of the opinion that in spite of many constitutional and social improvements, the 'Dalits' non-creamy layered, agricultural labourers, peasant women and those living below poverty line still suffer from triple oppression of caste, class and gender.

Mrs. Pradnya V. Ghodpade, in her paper, "Caste Conflict in Mulk Raj Anand's Major Novels" examines Mulk Raj Anand's major novels like *Untouchable, Coolie, The Big Heart* and *The Road*, which deal with the miserable lives of the downtrodden and poor outcaste society. She argues that almost all the protagonists of M.R. Anand belong to different castes/classes and they are victims of either caste/class conflict or victims of male-dominated social system. Dr. V. Thanuvalingam presents how the narrator, the second self of the author plays a significant role in evolving the fiction; how the narrative voice or the narrator takes omniscience over the fictional material — the character, events, incidents and episodes.

Hari Om Prasad's paper deals with Rabindra Nath Tagore as a novelist — such a novelist who made his characters natural, realistic and life-like; who represented the socio-religious culture of Bengal during the later half of the 19th century; who became a great champion of the cause of women's problems etc.

S.G. Bhanegaonkar in his scholarly paper on Kamala Markandaya's *Nectar in a Sieve* elegantly shows the symbolism of fertility *e.g.*, the descriptions of harvests and the brilliant analysis of motherhood, an indispensable part of womanhood. He thinks that Markandaya's *Nectar in a Sieve* extols the jubilant Mother Nature for all her wonderful creative achievements. It is the fertility which is the finest of all qualities that Nature and woman are endowed with.

Arjun Kumar presents an analytical criticism of the ironic vision engendered in the major novels of R.P. Jhabvala. In Nayantara Sahgal's *A Situation in New Delhi*, Dr. Chhote Lal Khatri focuses his entire attention on the political description of the novel. The novel, as he thinks, is not only an indictment against the Government's failure to formulate a new education but also against parents and teachers for not understanding their children and students.

Silence is a key metaphor which has several layers of meaning in Shashi Deshpande's *That Long Silence*. Silence which is suggestive of death and disaster, negates the self. This is what Arati Biswal observes in her scholarly paper, "Sound of the Silenced : Shashi Deshpande's *That Long Silence*." In "Her Life Is Her Own," Darshana Trivedi critically examines Shashi Deshpande's other novel, *The Dark Holds No Terror*. His paper is an attempt to study Saru's journey from alienation to self-realization, from diffidence to confidence. After facing individual crisis, finally Saru turns out to be an individual woman with the conviction and self-assertion : "My Life is My Own."

Dr. Sharda Iyer explicates Anita Desai's *In Custody* and shows how Deven Sharma, a temporary lecturer in Hindi has to face so many trials and tribulations, success and failure, enthusiasm and hesitance in his life. In the end, he finds strength in his inner self and resolves to face life.

Dr. Basavaraj Naikar judges Khushwant Singh's *I Shall Not Hear the Nightingale* as a novel of conflict between imperialism and nationalism, between the colonizer and the colonized. He also argues that apart from the colonial conflict depicted in the novel, there are other details which make the novelist a hard realist; a realist who has the courage to look into the face of harsh reality and depict it objectively without any sentimentalism or exaggeration. Dr. Ashok Kumar Bachchan beautifully interpretes fantasy, prophesy and real vision of Arun Joshi's *The City and the River*. He holds the opinion that whereas in the previous novels of Arun Joshi, fantasy and satire had been incidental, in *The City and the River*, these constitute the basic fictional technique.

Rama Kundu's "Seth's Use of Rhythm in *A Suitable Boy*," analyses objectively the three powerful images of the novel *e.g.*, the growth of a huge bunyan tree, the exposition of an Indian classical raag and the flow of the Ganga. She holds the view that these three images seem to hold the key to certain basic structural features of the novel and also pervade the texture and determine the mood, terror and effect like those of E.M. Forster in *A Passage to India*.

Arundhati Roy has become a prominent figure in the realm of English literature by writing her debut novel, *The God of Small Things*. This novel has got the prestigious Booker Prize and has been translated in almost all the major languages of the world. It presents, among other things, a miserable condition of the dalit and the deserted, the vulnerable and the marginalized. This is what we can see in the critical essay of M.B. Gaijan, who has tried his best to interpret the novel with the help of some Vedic concepts. Dr. John E. Abraham examines the novel objectively and presents a detail study. He holds the view that *The God of Small Things* is a flash of lightning which shocks and astonishes the reader for moment, and for a moment only.

In the last article which is on Taslima Nasrin's controversial novel, *Lazza*, I have made an attempt to examine the novel with reference to the history of religious satire. The aim of the paper is to present a sense of harmony and integration in a fanatically afflicted society where persecution and discrimination on the name of religion is on its summit.

I wish to record my obligation to all the contributors, who stretched their helping hand in making of this volume. I am also thankful to Prof. U.S. Rukhaiyar, Pro-Vice-Chancellor; Prof. Birendra Prasad Sinha, Retd. Principal; Prof. R.R. Dubey, former Head of the Department of English, Prof. Ranjit Singh, Principal, Jagdam College; Mr. Subodh Kumar Gupta & Mrs. Poonam Gupta, Vishakhapatnam and Mr. Saroj Kumar Gupta, Rourkela.

I am also richly indebted to my brothers Atma Ram Prasad and Triloki Nath Prasad, Bhagwanpur Hat (Siwan) and Sri Lal Babu Prasad Soni (Devi Jewellers), Sagarpur, New Delhi who, encouraged my spirit of editing the book. And lastly, a word of thanks is also due to Dr. K.R. Gupta, the Managing Director of M/s Atlantic Publishers and Distributors, New Delhi for publishing this book.

AMAR NATH PRASAD

CONTENTS

LIST OF CONTRIBUTORS

1. **AMAR NATH PRASAD**, Department of English, Jagdam College (J.P. University), Chapra-841 301 (Bihar).
2. **SURENDRA NARAYAN JHA**, Reader and Head, Department of English, M.K. College, Laheriasarai, Darbhanga (Bihar).
3. **N.D.R. CHANDRA**, Reader and Head, Department of English, Nagaland Central University, Kohima (Nagaland).
4. **MRS. PRADNYA V. GHORPADE**, Senior Lecturer, Arts & Commerce College, Ashta, Sangli (Maharashtra).
5. **V. THANUVALINGAM**, Reader in English, Annamalai University, Annamalai Nagar (Tamilnadu).
6. **HARI OM PRASAD**, Research Scholar, J.P. University, Chapra (Bihar).
7. **S.G. BHANEGAONKAR**, Lecturer, Post-Graduate Department of English, People's College, Nanded (Maharashtra).
8. **ARJUN KUMAR**, Lecturer in English, Rajendra College, Chapra (Bihar).
9. **CHHOTE LAL KHATRI**, Lecturer in English, S.S. College, Jehanabad (Bihar).
10. **ARATI BISWA**, L 20, Forest Park, Bhubaneshwar (Orissa).
11. **DARSHANA TRIVEDI**, School of Languages, Gujarat University, Ahmedabad (Gujarat).
12. **SHARADA IYER**, Department of English, Vasanta College for Women, Rajghat, Varanasi (U.P.).

13. **BASAVARAJ NAIKAR**, Professor of English, Karnataka University, Dharwad (Karnataka).

14. **ASHOK KUMAR BACHCHAN**, University Department of English, L.N. Mithila University, Darbhanga (Bihar).

15. **RAMA KUNDU**, Reader in English, P.G. Department, Burdwan University, Burdwan (W.B.).

16. **JOHN E. ABRAHAM**, C.M.S. College, Kottayam (Kerala).

17. **M.B. GAIJAN**, Lecutrer in English, Department of English, Samaldas Arts College, Bhavnagar (Gujarat).

1

Gandhian Impact on Indo-Anglian Fictions

—Amar Nath Prasad

> "...good writers are, so to speak, mediumistic to the deeper stirrings of life of their time while they are still unkonwn to, or at any rate unsuspected by, the public, politicians and current received opinion... Contemporary novels are the mirror of the age, but a very special kind of mirror, a mirror that reflects not merely the external features of the age but also its inner face, its nervous system, coursing of its blood and the unconscious promptings and conflicts which sway it."[1]
>
> *—Walter Allen*

INDO-ANGLIAN Fictions, particularly the fictions of the thirties, are immensely influenced by the ideals of Mahatma Gandhi, who fought for the cause of the under-privileged classes, the have-nots and the downtrodden, the marginalized and the defenceless. Apart from many other things, these writers have mirrored the various incidents and happenings of the life and activities of Mahatma Gandhi in particular and the contemporary social and political, economic and religious upheavals in general. But their works, as we shall see, are not simply the collection of historical facts or events; they are highly literary saturated with poetic grandeur and artistic craftsmanship. Among the works dealing with the theme of either Gandhi or the contemporary freedom struggle are Mulk Raj Anand's *Untouchable* (1935), Raja Rao's *Kanthapura* (1938),

K.S. Venkataramani's *Kandan the Patriot* (1932), D.F. Karaka's *We Never Die* (1944), Amir Ali's *Conflict* (1947), Venu Chitali's *In Transit* (1950), K.A. Abbas's *Inqilab* (1955), R.K. Narayan's *Waiting for the Mahatma* (1956), Nayantara Sahgal's *A Time to Be Happy* (1955), and K. Nagarajan's *Chronicles of Kedaram* (1961).

It is to be noted that one of the prime duties of a great writer is to represent the society and its various influences in his art. His work may be morbidly called *fin de siecle* if it fails to portray the spirit of the age. In other words, literature and society are interwoven both internally and externally; they are the two sides of the same coin. Why? Because the writer is the part and parcel of society. So, he is bound to reflect the zeitgeist or the spirit of the age. W.H. Hudson rightly holds the view :

"Literature is the vital record of what men have seen in life, what they have experienced of it, what they have thought and felt about those aspects of it which have the most immediate and enduring interest for all of us. It is, thus, fundamentally an expression of life through the medium of language...Man, as we are often reminded, is a social animal; and as he is thus by the actual constitution of his nature unable to keep his experiences, observations, ideas, emotions, fancies, to himself, but is on the contrary under stress of a constant desire to impart them to those about him."[2] And exactly this is what the novelists of the Gandhian Era did in their respective works mentioned above. A close study of their concerned works clearly reveal the fact that though they beautifully portray the contemporary movements, they are never devoid of the aesthetic functions of a great work of art. As a matter of fact, however rich and honest description of an event may be, it has no permanent significance in a piece of work of art unless it is woven into the fabric of art.

One of the salient features of Gandhian literature is the simplicity and clarity of language as Mahatma Gandhi strongly believed in the dictum — 'simple living and high thinking.' Perhaps this is why the writers of this age discarded ornateness, artificiality, pedantry and laborious artistry in their language both in English and in the vernaculars. In theme, the novelists preferred the village to the city, the poor to the rich, the cultural heritage of the village to the urban luxury and sophistication. Almost all the protagonists of these novels come from the lower class of society — a society afflicted with British imperialism, economic exploitation, recial discrimination, religious conflicts and above all political crisis. M.R. Anand points out :

"The warmth towards Bakha may have emerged from my warmth towards the person of Gandhi."[3] He further says that his life got a 'U' turn when he came in contact with the ideals of Mahatma Gandhi. Its impact was so immense that he began to wear home spuns clothes and decided writing "the poorest of the poor human beings whom I had known...specially was I inspired to brood on the castaways...And Gandhi also exhorted devotion to the poor."[4]

Mulk Raj Anand's first novel, *Untouchable* is absolutely influenced by M.K. Gandhi, a character in the novel, who appears in the last pages. The novelist presents a realistic picture of the one day life of the protagonist, Bakha, an untouchable boy who has to suffer abuse and rebuke, tyranny and injustice without any rhyme and reason — only because he belongs to untouchable class. In all the incidents — Temple Incident, Bazaar Incident, Hockey Match Incident, Well Incident, — the hero has to undergo untold humiliation and undeserved derogatory remarks flung by the high castemen. His long suppressed and tired soul mutters :

"Why we are always abused? The santry inspector that day abused my father. They always abuse us. Because we are sweepers. Because we touch dung. They hate dung. I hate it too. That is why I came here. I was tired of working on the latrines every day. That is why they don't touch us, the high castes."[5]

In the last pages of the novel, Mahatma Gandhi emerges as a Mesiah to uproot untouchability and caste-discrimination. Bakha felt delighted when Gandhi gives the appellation of 'Harijan,' sons of God to the 'bhangis and chamars.' Bakha is richly influenced by the words of Mahatma Gandhi who addresses the big gatherings :

"The fact that we address God as 'the purifier of the polluted souls' makes it a sin to regard anyone born in Hinduism — as polluted — it is satanic to do so. I have never been tired of repeating that it is a great sin. I don't say that this thing crystallised in me at the age of twelve, but I do say that I did then regard untouchability as a sin."[6]

Thus, the speech of Gandhi acts like the balm on the wounds of the protagonist, who longs for asserting his identity in a caste-dominated societal framework. It is his powerful speech that consoles his long suppressed heart flooded with remorse and despair. Now the ray of hope comes to his life and he feels a sense of emancipation and creativity. The author observes beautifully :

"The sun descended. The pale, the purple, the mauve of the horizon blended into darkest blue. A handful of stars throbbed in the heart of the sky. He emerged from the green of the garden into the slight haze of dust that rose from the road and the paths. As the brief Indian twilight came and went, a sudden impulse shot through the transformations of space and time, and gathered all the elements that were dispersed in the stream of his soul into a tentative decision : 'I shall go and tell father all that Gandhi said about us,' he whispered to himself, and what that clever poet said."[7]

Gandhian view also sets the tone of Raja Rao's first novel, *Kanthapura*, in which the tremors of Gandhi's influence can be felt more vigorously than in *Untouchable*. It deals with the powerful impact of Mahatma Gandhi on the villagers of a South Indian village. The story is narrated by an elderly widow in a very fine way. The manner of her telling the story is full of spontaneity and sweetness, irony and humour suffused with a deep touch of village atmosphere. Here, the political activities mostly related to Mahatma Gandhi are transcended and described in such a way that they become the part and parcel of Indian age-long myth and legend, history and religion, that is, "the hum-drum becomes the unique, the trivial becomes the heroic, and the hectic excitement of a day becomes a permanent communal possession.... the heroes and heroiness of epics jostle with historic personalities, and time past and time present are both projected into time future."[8]

The book is modelled on ancient puranas. It looks like a *Gandhi Purana* in which Moorthy represents the spirit of Gandhi, the Satyagrahi, the leader of the non-violent movement in Kanthapura. The cruel rule of the Britishers is the rule of the 'Danavas' in the religious scriptures. K.R.S. Iyengar observes :

"The characters sharply divide into two camps : the Rulers (and their supporters), on the one hand, and Satyagrahis (and their sympathisers), on the other. There are various other divisions too : orthodoxy is pitted against reform, exploitation against sufferance, the planter aganist the coolies, the corrupt officials aganist the self-respecting villagers. But these lines grow hazy when the main issue between the Bureaucracy and the Satyagrahis is joined, for now most people are on one or the other side of the barricades."[9]

Thus, *Kanthapura*, the *tour de force*, explicates the explicit attitude of Mahatma Gandhi, whose universal theory of truth and non-violence embalmed the wound of the poor and the deserted Indians. It tourniquetted the bleeding of the age-long suppression and oppression the Indians had to suffer sometimes on cause and sometimes without any cause. M.K. Naik aptly holds the view :

"*Kanthapura* is, thus, a brilliant attempt to probe the depths to which the nationalistic urge penetrated, showing how, even in the remote villages, the new upsurge fused completely with traditional religious faith, thus, rediscovering the Indian soul."[10]

K.S. Venkatramani's *Murgan the Tiller* and *Kundan the Patriot* bear a great witness to the Mahatma's impact. Murgan advocates the economic theory of Gandhi while Kundan, the political thoughts. In *Kundan the Patriot*, both the personal and the domestic things are mingled with the larger political issues. As a result, 'poetry, politics and prophesy mingle together in bewildering fashion'. The novel points out a number of things concerning the life of Mahatma Gandhi without actually introducing himself as a character as in *Untouchable*. The whole story revolves round the Civil Disobedience Movement of the nineteen thirties. It tells the story of Kundan, an Oxford-educated Indian youth. Mad with the emotion of patriotism, he resigns from the Indian Civil Service and plunges into the national movement. This episode reminds us of Sri Aurobindo and Subhash Chandra Bose who didn't succumb to the lure of the great service. We see that Kundan has a prophetic dream before he breathes his last. He makes a long patriotic speech tinged with the spirit of Gandhism.

Venu Chitale's *In Transit* also presents a beautiful picture of Indian history between two World Wars dominated by the ideals of Gandhi. It deals with the various ups and downs going on in the mind of the renascent India. It maintains "the right balance between the weight of tradition and the momentum of change and so calls for creative powers of a very high order, and hence it is no derogation of Venu Chitale's work to say that she has not succeeded — any more than Abbas has done."[11]

The novel, *Inqilab* by Ahmad Abbas shows not only Mahatma Gandhi, it also introduces some other personalities of the Gandhian age. It covers the incidents from the Rowlatt Bill and the Jallianwalla Bagh masacre to the Salt Satyagrah and the Gandhi-Irwin Pact of 1931. It projects the Gandhian ideals in its true perspective. Anwar, the protagonist of the novel goes from place to place gathering experiences of various kinds — political, religious and social. He goes to Muslim University at Aligarh where he fell in love with a Muslim girl, Salmah, the daughter of a professor of the University. He also comes in contact with a number of students — revolutionaries, congressmen, marxists and communalists. In course of time, he, alongwith some other student leaders, is expelled from the university because they took, like Jawaharlal Nehru, the Independence Pledge in the university campus on 26 Januray 1930. The consequence of this incident is so powerful that Salmah turns her face aganist Anwar and marries a Deputy Superintendent of Police. Now Anwar, free from the burden of domestic life, devotes himself fully to the cause of national movement. He travels all over India, accompanied by his friend, Robert, and sees how the people of India, particularly the neglected peasants, lead a miserable life beyond description; how the chain of events engendered by Mahatma Gandhi and other political leaders stir the minds of the unprivileged mass tyrannised by the Britishers. The novel ends with the tragic note of the exposure of the secret that Anwar is really an illegitimate son of a Hindu merchant who was brought up by a Muslim. On the political plane, the novel ends on the Gandhi-Irwin pact.

Amir Ali's famous novel, *Conflict* (1947) snaps the political upheavals as well as the sentiments of a Hindu family caught in the agitation of 1942. Shankar, a village boy, goes to Bomby for higher education. But, instead of education, he is caught in the agitation raised by Mahatma Gandhi and other leaders. He represents all those contemporary intellectuals who left their studies to join the national movement for freedom. In this novel, the novelist has also shown the rustic life of Indian which is enmeshed in the urban surroundings.

R.K. Narayan's *Waiting for the Mahatma*, as the title suggests, espouses, apart from other things, the assumptions or hypotheses of Gandhism. Here, the action strays out of Malgudi. The two central characters, Bharati and Sriram are 'existentially engaged in politics.' Sri Ram, a typical weak-willed character, and Bharati, a Congress volunteer devote themselves to national movement, though the hero is more interested in Bharati than in 'Bharat-mata'. K.R.S. Iyengar observes :

"Other novelists whether writing in English or in the regional languages, have likewise exploited the magic of Gandhi's name and presence, but seldom is the Gandhian role subsumed in the fiction as a whole. Gandhi is too big to be given a minor part : on the other hand, he is sure to turn the novel into a biography if he is given a major (or the central) part. The best thing for the contemporary novelist would be to keep Gandhi in the background but make his influence-felt indirectly."[12]

Thus, the book apparently portrays not only Gandhi's influences but also his appearances, *e.g.* his visit to Malgudi, his last prayer on 30 January 1948, the fatal day he was killed. But the author's art of fusing many themes into one doesn't seem successful. M.K. Naik seems to have rightly observed :

"If Narayan's main aim here was to depict the freedom struggle of 1942, his picture is neither representative nor evocative. Sriram's sudden conversion into a freedom fighter is unconvincing."[13]

Nayantara Sahgal, the daughter of Mrs. Vijyalakshmi Pandit and niece of Pt. Jawaharlal Nehru, in her very first novel, *A Time to be Happy*, deals with Congress activities and the movement of 1942 in an interesting way. The novelist is basically famous for her description of politics of the contemporary society. She was highly influenced by the ideals of Gandhi as well as Nehruism. The favourite theme of Nayantara Sahgal is political happenings, Indian women's search for sexual freedom, political turmoil outside and the individual's torment inside giving birth to broken promises and unsuccessful marriages etc. So far as the ideal or assumption of Gandhi is concerned, she may be seen both in her literary and personal life, a great champion for the cause of Gandhian attitude of life. In her own words :

"No single fact had done more to re-orient the thinking of an entire nation than Gandhi's semi-nakedness, It had shifted the political spotlight from town to village, jolting the town-dweller into an awareness of the peasant's existence and plight."[14]

We see that in most of her novels, Nayantara Sahgal pleads for the liberation and equality of social, political and personal life particularly the Indian women's urge to be considered as an equal partner of man in all the walks of life. This is exactly what Gandhi stands for. The novel, *A Time to be Happy*, shows how Sanad, the son of a zamindar, joins a British firm of Selkirk and Lowe and comes in contact with Western influences. He develops a habit of drinking. He marries Kusum, a worthy girl, who makes his life happy and so the title goes *A Time to Be Happy*.

K. Nagarajan's *tour de force*, *Chronicles of Kedaram* clearly points out the thoughts of Mahatma Gandhi, his intervention to unite the two Iyengar factions — the tengalai and the vadakalai. It presents a clash between the modernity and antiquity; a conflict between the West and the East; a confrontation between the possessed and the unprivileged; and above all, a dispute between the Hindu and the Muslim, the touchable and the untochable. The novelist seems to fling irony at the Iyengar feud. And perhaps this is why in order to calm down the tension between the two Iyengar sects, the author has deliberately introduced Mahatma Gandhi who got success in making them unite.

Mahatma Gandhi was a great apostle for the cause of the untouchable. He thought that untouchability is a great crime against man and God. It is a matter of great shame that in spite of his best efforts to eradicate untouchability from India, this dangerous disease still kills the people. This is what Arundhati Roy, depicts among other things in her famous book, *The God of small Things*, a Booker Prize Winner novel. The central character of the book, who symbolizes 'the God of Loss', the 'God of Small Things", or the 'Mombatti' is Velutha, an untouchable paravan in Kerala. He is an expert mechanic and craftsman. Perhaps this is why Mammachi employs him in her factory to do a carpenter's job. But the workers employed in the factory are not happy to see Velutha as a carpenter. Velutha is also seen taking part in political activity fighting for the cause of Marxism. He converts himself into the Christian religion only to be immune from the victimization of a casteist society. But his conversion and his technical expertise, apart from many other good things, never bring in fruitful result in the cruel and callous society. Velutha, alongwith his father, Velya, always goes to the Ayemenem House to deliver coconut plucked from the trees. But they are never allowed to enter the room. They were not permitted to touch a thing that a 'touchable touched.' Mammachi, Estha's grandmother, remembers a day "When paravans were expected to crawl backward with a broom, sweeping away their footprints so that the Brahmin and Christians wouldn't defile themselves by accidentally stepping into a paravan's footprint. In Mammachi time, paravans like other untouchables were not allowed to walk on public roads, not allowed to cover their upper bodies, not allowed to carry umbrellas. They had to put their hands over their mouths when they spoke to divert their polluted breath away from those whom they addressed."[15]

Arundhati Roy, a great champion of the cause of Gandhism, points out those unnoticed shades of the dalit and the deserted which generally escape the eyes of a social scientist. Velutha's grandfather Kelan, alongwith a number of other untouchable embraced Christianity to escape the scourge of untouchability. But they later on, found that they had committed a blunder. Though they were given separate churches and separate priests and in a special favour they were even given their own separate Pariah Bishop, but after 1947, they found they were not entitled to any government's benefits like job reservation nor bank loans at low interest. Why? Because they were Christians and so casteless. Roy says :

"It was little like having to sweep away your footprints without a broom. Or worse, not being allowed to leave footprints at all."[16]

In this novel, Arundhati Roy, like Mahatma Gandhi, is of the opinion that even a dalit or an untouchable can become an engineer or a doctor or a lawyer or a professor. Mammachi often said about Velutha that 'if only he hand't been a paravan, he might become an engineer.'[17] As a matter of fact, God never makes any difference between a touchable and an untouchable; between the poor and the rich; between the sordid and the sublime. The minds of all men are almost equal. The thing which is needed is to appreciate and to provide proper facilities to the down-trodden and the underdogs. The obscure living can't and shouldn't be condemned. The deserted and the defenceless people are the significant competent of the nation in the sense that they work honestly. The economy of the country cannot remain in its key without the co-operation of the dalit and the downtrodden. They, thus, can't be consigned to oblivion. Thomas Gray rightly observes :

> "Full many a gem of purest ray serene
> The dark unfathomed caves of ocean bear;
> Full many a flower is born to blush unseen
> And lost its fragrance in the desert air."[18]

Thus, this brief survey tries to show that Mahatma Gandhi came into the limelight not only on the pages of history and social sciences but also in literature — both in English and the other vernaculars. He gave to the world a new doctrine — a new way of giving expression to people's demands and claims; a new strength and inspiration to unarmed masses. He spiritualized politics by his strict adherence to the doctrine of truth and non-violence. His powerful impact on the socio-political scene of the 1930s, particularly on the Indo-Anglian literature is immense. Most of the masterpieces of Indo-Anglian novelists *e.g.*, Mulk Raj Anand, R.K. Narayan and Raja Rao wouldn't have been able to see the light of the day, if Gandhi hadn't exercised his influences on these authors.

NOTES AND REFERENCES

1. Allen. Walter, *Reading a Novel*, pp. 18-19. Quoted by P.P. Mehta, *Indo-Anglian Fictions — An Assessment,* Bareilly, 1948, pp. 92-93.
2. Hudson, William Henry, *An Introduction to the Study of Literature*, Kalyani Publishers, Ludhiana, reprint, 1986, p. 10.
3. Anand, M.R. "Why I Write," *Kakatiya Journal of English Studies*, Vol. II, No. 1. Spig., 1977, p. 255.
4. *Ibid.*, p. 15.
5. Anand, M.R., *Untouchable*, Arhold Heinemann, reprinted 1984, New Delhi, p. 58.
6. *Ibid.*, p. 164.
7. *Ibid.*, pp. 175-76.
8. Iyengar, K.R.S., *Indian Writing in English*, Sterling Publishers Private Ltd., New Delhi, Reprint 1994, p. 390.

9. *Ibid.*, p. 391.
10. Naik, M.K., *A History of Indian English Literature*, Sahitya Akademi, New Delhi, 1999, p. 167.
11. Iyengar, K.R.S., *Indian Writing in English, op. cit.*, p. 286.
12. *Ibid.*, p. 372.
13. Naik, M.K., *A History of Indian English Literature, op. cit.*, p. 165.
14. Sahgal, Nayantara, *From Fear Set Free,* Orient Paperbacks, New Delhi, p. 25.
15. Roy, Arundhati, *The God of Small Things*, India Ink. Publishing Co. Pvt. Ltd., New Delhi, 1997. pp. 73-74.
16. *Ibid.*, p. 74.
17. *Ibid.*, p. 75
18. Gray, Thomas, "Elegy Written in a Country Churchyard," Palgrave's *Golden Treasury* (Oxford University Press, Calcutta), 1964, p. 146.

2

The Reflection of Socio-political Changes in the Indian English Fiction : Between 1935 and 1975

—Surendra Narayan Jha

ALTHOUGH Indian English fiction has to struggle a lot to establish itself, the recent acclaim won by Vikram Seth (*A Suitable Boy*) and Arundhati Ray (*The God of Small Things*) has put it in global gaze. But, its long strife for due recognition can be easily understood by some adverse comments it received all along in its way to success. Although himself a man of Indian origin, V.S. Naipaul calls Indian English Fiction "a mimicry of the West."[1] John Wain, the contemporary poet-critic of England, goes even further by blaming the whole gamut of Indian English writers as having "an insecure grip on the idiom"[2] of English.

Yet, despite these negative comments, Indian English fiction has treaded a long way. With some really brilliant achievements, prof. M.K. Naik goes to the extent of remarking that "one of the most notable gifts of English education to India is prose-fiction, for though India was probably the fountain-head of story-telling, the novel as we know today was an importation from the West."[3] Of course, Indian English fiction has a clear beginning in Bankim Chandra Chaterjee's *Rajmohan's Wife* (1864), its real presence was felt after half a century later by the almost simultaneous emergence of the great trinity — Mulk Raj Anand, R.K. Narayan and Raja Rao, all of them began writing novels around mid-1930s. Bhabani Bhattacharya was also a contemporary of these novelists by birth, but he started writing fiction just after the Indian independence.

This study takes up the undercurrent of East-West encounter culminating abudantly in socio-political changes sweeping all over India in those critical years just before and after the independence as reflected in some of the major novels of those four important novelists. For a focused critical study, I have selected *Untouchable* (1935), *Coolie* (1936), *Two Leaves and a Bud* (1937), and *The Old Woman and The Cow* (1960) by Mulk Raj Anand; *Waiting for the Mahatma* (1955), *The Guide* (1958), *The Vendor of Sweets* (1967) and *The Painter of Signs* (1976) by R.K. Narayan; *Kanthapura* by Raja Rao and *So Many Hungers* (1947), *Music for Mohini* (1952), *He who Rides a Tiger* (1952), *A Goddess Named Gold* (1960) and *Shadow from Ladakh* (1966) by Bhabani Bhattacharya.

Mulk Raj Anand is the Indian version of Charles Dickens as far as the treatment of social theme is concerned. He is a messiah of the downtrodden, with "understanding compassion for the waifs, the disinherited, the lowly, the lost."[4] The first three novels of Anand deal with such wretchedly poor protagonists as Bakha, Munoo and Gangu. *Untouchable* minutely features almost all the events of a single day in the life of the low-caste boy, Bakha. Thus, the author intends that a radical change in relation to Indian social fabric is quite at hand, and it would by and large dispel the pall of gloom and usher in a casteless and classless society. While, his *Coolie* tenders rather a cross-section of India more like the microcosm that is Indian society. Despite widespread evil, Munoo appears to be all the more convinced that the root of the matter is poverty only. In fact, Anand likes to infer that it is like a poison that infects all our society and makes it sordid and inhuman in the long run. While Anand mostly glorifies, eleswhere, certain benevolent influences the British rule had on the then India. In *Two Leaves and a Bud* greatly denounces the evil aspects of its impact most ruthlessly. Here, Gangu, a middle-aged peasant from a village near Hoshiarpur in the Punjab who has lost his land and hut to greedy money-lenders is easily lured by fabulous promises of Buta, the Coolie-catcher, takes his family to Macpherson Tea Estate in Assam. Soon after his arrival, Gangu realizes that he has unwillingly walked into a trap. Because forced to work in unhygienic condition and starved, he is shot dead by a British officer, who tries to rape his daughter. What the author mainly intends to objectify is the British attitude to the Indian and how it can be both imperialistic as in the case of Reggie Hunt or liberal as in that of Dr. de la Havre. The last novel of this study by Anand takes up the plight of Gauri, a destitute peasant woman who fights her way to financial independency free from the tyranny of her husband and society as well. It truly unfolds Anand's usual crusade aganist man's belief in superstition, karma, and God — all age-old ideas which exactly mar man's progress. The author, thus vividly portrays the wretched condition of Indian women in rural atmosphere, and suggests the changes that are coming about by furnishing a lively account of the heroine's enlightened reaction to tradition and custom corrupted through man's selfishness, ignorance and vested interests.

Waiting for the Mahatma by R.K. Narayan depicts the freedom struggle aganist the background of Gandhi's role in it, interwoven with a beauatiful love story between Sriram and Bharati. While in *Untouchable* Gandhi appears only towards the end, in this novel his role is more frequent and functional. On the whole. it is Bharati who makes a patriot and a noble soul of Sriram. In marriage, therefore, he is sure to find in her his redemption. His *The Guide* also presents more or less Gauri-like miserable predicament of a woman. However, Rosie is not only educated but a famous dancer *par excellence*. Yet, she has to suffer exploitation by both her husband and her lover before she frees herself from their clutches. This novel opens with Raju in the dilapidated village temple reverantially accepted as a Sadhu and also ends in the same surroundings with the hero's enforced death. Besides, it poses several pertinent questions with regard to human motives and actions. Rather, it comples one to brood over reality and appearance, the man and the mask, ends and means, etc. The Gandhi motif again comes in *The Vendor of Sweets*. Here, Jagan, a sweet seller, is very much concerned at the Westernisation of his only son, Mali. But, the latter administers shock upon shock to his father. The frustrated Jagan ultimately renounces the world and takes delight in watching a goddess come out of stone. Naturally, he authorises his cousin, his own *alter ego*, to take necessary steps with respect to Mali's arrest even. In *The Painter of Sign*, Narayan returns to the role and freedom of woman in the Indian society. The relationship between Raman, the Young, unattached sign-painter and Daisy of the Family planning Centre goes through vicissitudes. It finally makes him lose both his aunt (who, disapproving of the match, goes on a pilgrimage) and would be wife. The Raman-Daisy relationship recalls that between Sriram and Bharati in *Waiting for the Mahatma*. However, Daisy is a highly advanced copy of Rosie of *The Guide*. For long Rosie has to dance to the tune of her husband and her lover, but Daisy makes her lover, Raman, Dance to her own tune right from the beginning.

Kanthapura by Raja Rao is widely acknowledged as "perhaps the finest evocation of the Gandhian age in Indian English Fiction."[5] It is the story of the Struggle of a south Indian village influenced for the first time by the Gandian principle of freedom. The story told by an old woman, Rangamma highlights the Gandhian agitation launched by Moorthy in the village. What gives this novel an eternal Indian appeal is its narrative technique of the Indian puranas or the Harikathas, mixing freely narration, description, reflection, religious discourse, folk-lore, etc. It is so absorbing and demonstrating that in the novel we observe everything through the film of the narrator's memory, sensibility and temperment. For this reason, even K.R. Srinivas lyengar calls this novel "a veritable grammar of Gandhian myth — the myth that is but a poetic translation of the reality."[6]

The early novels of Bhabani Bhattacharya are written aganist the backdrop of Bengal's dehumanising famine. In *So Many Hungers*, there is a graphic and poignant description of Bengal's suffering during the great famine of the early forties. Indeed, the novel obviously touches upon the theme of exploitation — political, economic and social. It really accounts for "a largely man-made hunger that took a toll of two million innocent men, women and children in Calcutta and Bengal."[7] This social theme is presented with the political effect of the Quit-India Movement. No Doubt, this novel is a deliberate impeachment of man's inhumanity to man. Alongwith, it produces a dramatic study of a set of human beings trapped in a unique tragic predicament. His second novel, *Music for Mohini*, deals with Bengal's backwardness and revelas how that is partly removed by the efforts of Jayadeva well supported by his wife, Mohini. It features the story of a Calcutta-born Brahmin girl, Mohini. She is a popular radio artiste who is later married to

Jayadeva, a scholar and writer with origin in his native village, Behula. Between Jayadeva and Mohini, there figures the perversity of the stars, the obsession of a mother and the fierce resentment of Sudha, a beautiful and intelligent girl with a grievance of her own. Out of the expected clash between the old and the new emerges a creative synthesis which culminates in splendid music, a sigificant matter of harmonising different notes. The poverty and suffering of Bengal, as depicted in his first novel, comes again in Bahttachraya's *He Who Rides A Tiger*. Here, the author switches over from a remote village, Behula to a metropolitan city, Calcutta. The tempo of life in this metropolitan city of India — the complex of urban vices and the thin veneer of urban sophistication, the pressure of mass movements and mass hysteria, the reign of superstition really constitue the piquant quality of the novel. Like *So Many Hungers*, the novel tells the story of Kalo, a poor blacksmith, driven by hunger to Calcutta, who is jailed for some time for stealing a bunch of bananas. His pitiable condition compels him to become a pimp to eke out a miserable livelihood. Further, he notices that his only daughter, Lekha, has herself been lured to one of the harlot-houses in his range. Though he succeeds in saving her just in time, the incident actually opens his eyes to the sordidness of the game. Right from here, Kalo declares war on society and resolves hard to strike at "the pillars for the famine they have caused and the harlort-houses they have kept flourishing."[8] The special theme of suffering because of the presence of some sharks in the society is the theme of *A Goddess Named Gold*. Undoubtedly this novel shows its affiliation with *So Many Hungers* and *He Who Rides a Tiger*, but in no way it can be taken the repetition of either. As a matter of fact, it greatly displays an advance in Bhattacharya's art as a novelist. Here, a greedy Seth, Samsundarji, makes an innocent girl like Meera his instrument of amassing wealth. *Shadow from Ladakh* is a typical novel set aganist the background of the Chinese invasion of 1962. It is a grand combination of both social and Political themes. This novel "contrasts the Gandhism of Satyajit Sen of Gandhigram with the scientism of Bhaskar, Chief Engineer of Steel town."[9] Finally, the conflict resolves by itself in the beautiful harmony of Sunita, the only child of Satyajit who falls in love with Bhaskar.

The presentation of socio-political changes in the major Indian English fiction discussed above is in no way less significant than that in the novels of Charles Dickens. The issues taken up by Dickens in his novels becmae instrumental in the enactment of certain reforms such as the Prison Reforms. Similarly, the issues raised by Mulk Raj Anand have also influences the Indian political thinkers to launch a tirade against untochability and other social disparities. The importancre given to the dignity of the complete man is the thematic concern of the novelists. Mulk Raj Anand in his first novel *Untouchable* (1935) deals with the role of Gandhi in eradicating the problem of untouchability arising out of caste hierarchy and the job of sweepers and scavengers cleaning night soil. In *Coolie* (1936) and *Two Leaves and a Bud* (1937) again the novelist deals with another class of under-privileged. Anand has also dealt with the freedom movement in *Untouchable* as well as *The Road* (1963) and *The Death of Hero* (1964).

R.K. Narayan has also dealt with the common socio-political problems prevailing in the country during his time. *Waiting for the Mahatma* (1955) and *The Vendor of Sweets* (1967) are novels on the Gandhian motif. Raja Rao again takes up almost the identical motif in his *Kanthapura* which he wrote before the Indian independence. Raja Rao's later works of fiction are metaphysical and philosophical problems in almost all his novels except *A Dream in Hawaii* (1978). *So Many Hungers* (1947) treats, among many other hungers, the hunger for freedom in the background of the *Quit India Movement* and the Bengal famine. *Music for Monini* (1952) is a novel of domestic compromise between horoscope and microscope, tradition and modernity, superstition and science, besides being an exploration of East-West encounter. *He who Rides a Tiger* (1952) and *Goddess Named Gold* (1960) continue with the treatment of social realism prevailing in West Bengal during the time. In *Shadow from Ladakh* (1966) Bhattacharya comes out of West Bengal and deals with the theme of Gandhism of Satyajit Sen of Gandhigram and scientism of Bhaskar, Chief Engineer of Steel Town. The two girls in Bhaskara's life, Sunita and Rupa, represent in turn the spinning wheel and the turbine respectively.

REFERENCES

1. Quoted by C.D. Narasimhaiah, *The Function of Criticism in India* (Mysore : Central Institute of Indian Languages, 1986), p. 169.
2. Quoted by Raja Ram Mehrotra, "Indian English : some Myths & Misconceptions," in Krishna Nandah Sinha ed. *Indian Writing in English* (New Delhi : Heritage, 1979), p. 195.
3. *Dimensions of Indian English Literature* (New Delhi : Sterling, 1985), p. 99.
4. K.R. Srinivas lyengar, *Indian Writing in English* (New Delhi : Sterling, 1985), p. 332.
5. M. K. Naik, *A History of Indian English Literature* (New Delhi : Sahitya Akademi, 1982), p. 166.
6. *Indian Writing in English*, p. 396.
7. *Ibid.*, p. 412-13.
8. *Ibid.*, p. 417.
9. M. K. Naik, *A History of Indian English Literature* (New Delhi : Sahitya Akademi, 1982), pp. 215-16.

3

"Identity, Culture & Theory; Towards Feminine Gender Representation"

—*Dr. N.D.R. Chandra*

1. Introduction

IDENTITY is concerned with the self-esteem and self-imagae of an individual, a gender, a community, a class, a race or sex or a nation — real or imaginary — dealing with the existence and role : who are we? What position do we have in spciety *vis-a-vis* international arena? So far as sex and gender identities are concerned, these are the quest for equality and dignity for their progress and development. The multiple identities of women, distribution of their gender roles in distinct and dominant cultures *i.e.*, the U.S. and India and their reflection of class position have been discussed here. In a sense, an attempt has been made to situate both the images of women in two distinct cultural contexts and theories therof.

Further, it is believd and aesthetic value is not universal, uniform, constant or eternal; it does not reside fully within the text. Rather, it is culturally and historically specific, produced in the act of reading. It is the materialist analysis of literature or politics which should offer a real possibility for women who are 'Dalits,' disadvantaged, disabled, non-white, lesbian of working class. "If the critic believes that race, sexual orientation or class are important constituents of writing the theory and criticism which recognize difference and represent more than a small privieged of women become possible" (Engleton, 1994 : 4).

2. National Identity in Multicultural Countries like the U.S. and India

In a multicultural country, the state is responsible for the preservation and security of all the minorities, marginalized groups and ethnic identities. These groups can participate in the development functions of society and the nation which is known as participationist pluralism. On the other hand,. they have to maintain the national unity. In multicultural countries like the U.S. and India, the identities such as, nation, language, caste, race, gender and sex are culturally specific despite their similarities. The American concept of National Identity rejects the basic European ideas *i.e.,* ethnic homogeneity and single language. So it is based on plurality. Whosoever has settled in America has become part and parcel of the country. In this sense, the U.S. is a 'Melting Pot' of different races, a silent crucible for making compound through chemical reaction. Here individuals of all nations are melted into a new race of men, whose labours and posterity will one day cause chages in the world" (Spanckeren, USIS : 18). America has now an integrated society and its citizens are held together by common aspirations to progress themselves and their country not by ethnicity or single language but by common will. "So the U.S. is a forward looking and expansive nation. It has to be built with the sense of patriotism, inheritance, legacy, a common ambition and aspirations" (Gopal, 1993: Tape).

Unlike Americans, our project of nationhood has to deal with the difficult terrain of "our golden past." It is particularly exhausting because we do not have a homogeneous history. It is a diverse past of many religions, many languages and many people. The Americans solved their problems of diversity by throwing their many immigrant communities into the 'melting pot.' Their ethnic immigrant minorities did not form separatist movements: they eagerly embraced the English language and the American way of life (Das, 1977 : 10.) They believe in the present and the future while we are lost in our 'glorious past.' In India, we historically tried to deal with our problem of diversity through caste system. The minorities became subcastes (Mandal Commission on Reservation Policy). But there are minorities such as Muslims who are the product of a proud universal religion and are willing to be assimilated as subcastes. Yet the attempt to solve the problem through caste system seems to be difflcult. Any way, if Americans are a 'melting pot' we are a mosaic. A good mosaic has a unit of style. In this sense, India's unity is provided by its civilization and the Indian way of life *i.e.*, Indianness (Das, 1977 : 10). In other words, we believe that India has unity in diversity. The very diversity of culture, race, caste, creed and language is a rainbow of Indianness where our national identity lies. In short, Indian is a land of Cultural Pluralism. It's the right time of nation building and different identities are expected to enrich their creative faculties in the cultural realm of Indian which will in turn, contribute to the process of nation-building.

The post-independence India experienced varied identity formation as a consequence of the process of industrialization, urbanization, globalization and expansion of the information technology. The identities that emerged were based on discrete received categories such as religion, Caste (Jati), Class (Verna), gender and sex (Patel, 1985 : 235). These varied identities do not suggest any uniform identity as they come from different socio-economic political fabric of India, and sometimes they are identified on the basis of suppression, oppression and exploitation. Though, the construction of a uniform homogenous identity was initiated during the period of the colonial and nationalist movement but these groups are yet to achieve the desired goals of political space for which they have been struggling for. Again, Americans are able to convert their independence into freedom, India is still experimenting democracy and sometimes it tends to be mobocracy and not the rule of law. However, both the countries have vision of pluralism which is in a way combination of assimilation and difference and representation of diverse groups. Identity, theory and gender representation are socially and culturally different though, they share some common assumptions, and therefore, they are the part of cultural studies.

3. Identity of Women

The beginning of identity politics emerged in the form of feminist and civil rights movement which proliferated through various identities — national, ethnic, somatic, sexual, gender and so on. The feminine gender identity is an enquiry into the multiplicity of cultural practice particularly of discourse and representations in relation to power. It is a post modern paradigm or anti-paradigm. It is self-assertion which is grounded in experience of inability, deprival, disability and disadvantaged. Today, feminists have been claiming separate identity on all fronts. So the Women's movement across the world has shifted from Women's emancipation to women's empowerment in human interest. While the Western radical feminist fought for 'sexual orientation' and free sex, the feminist movement in the developing countries is primarily based upon the socio-economic issues, such as, high mortality rate, female infanticide, bride-burning, dowry, violence aganist women, rape, suicides, adverse working conditions, rising inflation and so on. In fact. their struggle comes within the socio-economic and cultural fabric of the partriarchal society.

Women's movement in India has many divergences within itself. The urban elite women are quite aware of their rights while rural women are almost untouched with the feminist movement. Again, in urban area, the movement is dominated by the upper class but 'Dalits', non-creamy layered OBC, SC, ST agricultural labourers, peasant women, and those living below poverty line suffer from triple oppression of caste, class and gender. The concept like gender equality and emancipation are just dream which will never be realized in their life time. However, there is an awakening in rural based feminists which is different from the urban autonomous feminists and the party women wings. The rural women are also turning to find a genuinely self-reliant agriculture. The whole economy in India is moving towards Western capitalist model and towards information age, therefore, a chage in the socio-economic and cultural fabric of India especially in feminist perspectives cannot be ruled out.

Indian woman's identity is one that is usually connected to and defined by the societal and cultural norms of a practicable familial structure,. This identity is defined within the parameters of their social relationship to men. They are traditional, conservative, and therefore, they are reluctant to cross the 'Laxman rekha' of their family and culture. They are regarded as the preserver of essential nationalist spirit. They are to smile always, welcome their guests and enteratain them, care for their family members performing all the household responsibilties and if there is any pain, they are to hide it behind their veil. They are to become true symbol of Indian tradition and culture. Thus, Indian women becomes a metaphor for purity, chastity and sanctity of the ancient spirit that is India. The national construct of the Indian woman attributes the spiritual qualities of self-sacrifice, devotion, religiosity and so on. To family, which then stands as a sign for nation. Consequently, anything that threatens to dilute this model of Indian womanhood, constitutes a betrayal of all that it stands for : Nation, religion, god, the spirit of India, culture, tradition, and family (Bhattacharjee, 199 : 238).

The family and nation denote eternal, sacred and natural ties for national reconstructs; 'Nation-ness' therefore becomes the most legitimate value in the political life of our time (Andherson, 1991 : 3.5) "In this respect, the woman who occupies the space outside the heterosexual, patriarchal family is in a space unrecpognised by the nation, currently a highly valued construct. The displacement of her history is crucial for the construction of a nation; in re-claiming her voice, her story, she risks displacing the nation" (Bhattacharjee, 199 : 247).

It is believed that Indian women in general have no identity of their own. They belong to their father before they are married and to their husband after they are married and in the old age they have to depend on their sons. However, urban and metropolis educated Indain women, immigrants and expatriates are claiming their rights within their family and beyond it. They are attempting to establish a new identity with their changing gender roles. For example, in a conservative family, a husband used to represent in public affairs. Now most of elite young women represent and manage the public and political affairs. These identities of women are separate from their husband. Further, the working women particularly are to compromise and adjust themselves as wife, mother, as an employee performing their household traditional responsibilities and doing all the purchasing at market place too.

The rural women are generally confined within four walls. If needy women go to work, generally they are not employed and if they are employed, they lowly paid compared to their male counterparts. Very often, they are physically, sexually and orally exploited. So the sexual harassment is becoming common to both rural and urban areas. Women, in Indian society are segmented into more or less two warring groups every where; such as the conservative/liberal, rural/urban, 'Dalits/upper class, dependent/ independent, uneducated/educated, powerless/powerful, unprivileged/ privileged, and finally exploited/unexploited. Women, therefore, have to raise their voice for their rights particularly legal rights and substantial amd proportionate representatations in all walks of life eliminating their ignornace and indifference towards their rights. In fact, there is no much consciousness in Indian women, they are still backwards leaving a few elite urban women. Their position has changed little, thterefore, by and large, Indian society remains male-dominated.

In Indian context, Christian and Parsi women enjoy more freedom as compared to their Muslim and Hindu counterparts because of their socio-cultural beliefs. Tribal woman like Naga, Khasi, Garo and Nair women in Kerala have almost individual autonomy and they enjoy more freedom. Again, while in Hindu Society, social stratification, hierarchies, undeclared ban on intercaste and widow marriage, untouchability, segregation on the basis of religion, caste, creed and beliefs, illiteracy are some of the reasons of their backwardness. Moreover, the distinction berween rich and poor, employed and unemployed, privileged and unprivileged, haves and have-nots are aggravating their condition. Their toil and labour are neither recognized nor are they paid properly for their labour, particularly the labourers working in agricultural sectors and those doing household works. Therefore, they have to depend on their menfolks.

4. Changing Feminine Gender Roles & Identity

H.L. Mencken predicted in the early part of the twentieth century that more and more sexual restrictions would be relaxed, especially those affected the ablest women. He foresaw that a substanital number of them would concentrate on careers, allowing their sexual satisfaction to be temporary and changeable on careers much like the satisfaction enjoyed by many men (Mencken, 1990 : 59). However, most women are proud of their ability to bear children. The special aura that glorifies the pregnant woman has figured largely in the art and literature of both the East and the West (The most beautiful and mysterious smile of Monalisa is said to have been a pregnant woman). There will be a compromise in postponemnet of children rather than childlessness. Men and women today are often torn in conflict between a commitment to career and commitment to children. In future, many couples will sidestep this problem deferring the entire task of raising children until after retirement. Alvin Toftler, in his book entitled the *Future Shock* foretells that :

> Childless marriage, professional parenthood, post-retirement child-rearing, corporate families, communes, geriatric group marriage, homosexual family with which innovative minorities will experiment in the decades ahead. Not all of us, however, will be willing to participate in such experimentation what of the majority? (Tofler, 1971 : 219-38).

Further, he asserts today many women go to work when they finish raising children, tomorrow many will reverse that pattern, work first and child rearing next. This particular phenomenon along with the others is chaging the gender roles and therefore, feminine gender identity and representations are being remodelled. Hochschild in her book *The Second Shift* has categorized three types of ideologies of marital roles that arc based on the sphere — home or work — that the women wish to identify or be identified with, and the amount of power she wants to have less, more or equal in the relationship. These ideologies are categorised as traditional, transitional and Egalitarian (Sangeeta, 1999 : 58). Most of the urban especially working women are struggling to create a distinct self or an identity within their family and beyond it. They are in transitional stage. They feel that their husband should share their household work. In reality, in India, there are husbands who want to marry educated working women but they do not like to share the houshold responsibilities. Most of us therefore, are in transitional stage because they do not treat their wives as their equal partners. Further, the whole world is moving towards democratization. In "cosmospolitan societies in India, particulary educated women, are preferring love marriage claiming their identities like American European women, entering into new fields like media, film, and armed forces and standing by their boy-friends" (Marwah-Roy, 1999 : 27).

5. Feminist Literary Theory

Various women's movements through the passage of time activated and intensified the discussion of feminism in a academies and dynamized and generated changes in feminist theory, parctices and politics. Modern Feminist Criticism is deeply indebted to two writers, Virginia Woolf and Simone de Beauvoir. Their criticism exemplifies the strength as well as the challenge of literary feminism in its determination to go two ways at once (a) towards a feminist social critique or an analysis of women attempting to write in a patriarchal culture and (b) towards the development of feminist aesthetic, or an explanation of how writing by women manifests a distinctively female discourse. Further, Simone de Beauvoir in her book *The Second Sex* (1949) criticized patriarchal culture and analysed the marginal position of women in society and the arts. She identifies a Marxist brand of analysis grounded on political and economic oppression of women with a kind of "superstructure" of sexist literature and art. Thus, she conceived literature as reflection or imitation of social reality. There is some sort of similarity between Marxist and Feminist approaches as both of them adopt a 'conflict' model of society. Our individual roles and identities are not the outcome of a unified culture and an organic social process but are produced by a fundamentally unjust and oppressive social organization. "Marxist believe that human-self-realization is blocked by class domination at every level (economic, political and ideological). Feminists perceive women as in the position of a social class exploited by patriarchy at all levels (economic, political, ideological)" (Selden, 1989 : 135).

There is universal patterning in the representation of women in literature and art. To approach such a universal patterning, Showalter propounds a theory of criticism in her anthology *The New Feminist Criticism* (1986). She asserts that one of the earliest *manifestations* of feminist criticism concentrated on exposing the misogymy of literary practice: the stereotyped images of women in literature as angels or monsters, the literary abuse of textual harassment of women in classic and popular male literature, and the exclusion of women from literay history. The second phase of feminist criticism according to her focused on texts produced by women with a view to revising traditionally male determined literary history. The first is known as 'Phallocentrism', while the second approach is said to be 'gynocentrism.' Helenc Cixous combines the categories of women as a reader and as a writer and calls it as 'Phallologocentrism. "It offers a practice of wirting that aims to do this by passing plurality aganist unity; multitudes of meanings aganist single, fixed meaning; diffuseness aganist instrumentality; openness aganist closure." This disclosure is known as "structural" and a vision born of shifts, contraries, negations, contradictions; linked to personal vulnerability and need" (Davis, 1988 : 452).

Showalter describes theories of women's writing which make use of four models of difference : biological, linguistic, psychoanlytic and cultural. So Feminist theory of criticism involves multi-faceted critical approach such as Marxist, psychological and psycho-analytical, the structuralist and the global metaphysical vision of the antimetaphysics of post-structuralism and deconstruction. J. Hillis Miller also describes almost the similar type of feminist criticism in his essay entitled "The Search for Grounds in Literary Study" *viz.,* (1) a societal or social ground, the more or less hidden social or ideological pressures which impose themselves on literature, (2) a psychological ground, the more or less hidden psychic pressures which impose themselves on a work of literature, (3) a linguistic ground, the more or less hidden rhetorical pressure, or pressure from...language itself as such and finally (4) an almost inarticulate ground, which Miller calls properly religious, metaphysical, or ontological, though hardly in traditional or conventional way.

In the postmodern age the multiple feminine gender identity across the culture gives substance to the idea of sisterhood, it does so at the cost of differences among sisters. Although the theory allows for some differences among women of different classes, races, sexual orientations and ethnic groups, it construes these subsidiary to more basic similarities. However, the emergence of Women's Studies in academies has sown the seed of concrete inquiry with more limited aims constructing of the categories of sexuality and their problems. Thomas Docherty announcing the theory of postmodern-feminist project states :

> Post-modern-feminist theory would be non-universalist. When its focus becomes cross-cultural or transepochal, its mode of attention would be

> comparativist rather than universalizing, attuned to changes and contrasts instead of to covering laws. Finally, postmodern-feminist theory would dispense with the idea of subject; of history. It would replace unitary notions of women and feminine gender identity with plural and complexily constructed conceptions of social identity, treating gender as one relevant strand among others, attending also to class, race, ethnicity, age and sexual orientation (1993 : 429)

It is, therefore, said that the contemporary and postmodern feminist theroy is a pluralistic, inclusive, complex and multilayered feminist solidarity. It is essential for overcoming the oppression of women in its endless variety and monotonous similarity which is useful for contemporary feminist political practice too. Such practice is increasingly a matter of alliances rather than one of a unity around a universally shared interest or identity. It recongnizes that the diversity of women needs experiences. This means that no single solution, on issues like child care, social security and housing can be adequate for all. Thus, some women share some common interests and face some common enemies, such commonalities are by no means universal; rather they are interlaced with differences, even with conflicts. So the contemporary theory would look more like a tapestry composed of threads of many different hues than one women in a single colour" (Docherty, 1993 : 429).

6. Towads Feminine Gender Representation

Richard Johnson argues that there are three main forms of research in Cultural Studies : (a) the study of the processes of cultural production, (b) text-based approaches which focus on the cultural products themselves and (c) Research into lived cultures, which has been closely associated with a politics of representation. Further, Johnson recognizes a debt to feminist theory, which recognized into question of all kinds of assumption about literary and cultural history and about the relationship between the private self and the public sphere of activity (Johnson, 1986 : 277-314). In the similar manner, the interdisciplinary movement known as "feminist cultural studies" examinied three interrelated problems *i.e.*, productions, distribution and consumption : (i) The production of gendered, ethnic, political, cultural meanings, (ii) the textual analysis of these meanings and (iii) the study of lived cultures and lived experiences and their connections to these worlds of representation. The representations of women's experience as givesn in the mas media, film, social science, art, literature, politics and religion constitute critical layer of materials to be interpreted. In fact, the production, distribution and consumption of cultural meanings involve issues of ideology and political economy of signs (such as the *Good House Keeping*) and series on the neo-traditional woman), including how these signs are worded, photographed, where they circulate, who buy them, and so on. The Textual analysis of meanings require the implementation of variety of reading strategies (feminist, semiotic, hermeneutic, psychoanalytic) which examine how a text constitues (hails) an individual as a subject in a particular ideoogical moment and site. At the level of lived experiences, a central problem becomes the examiniation of how interacting individuals connect their lives during moments of upheaval and epiphany, to these ideological texts and make sense of their experience in terms of their meaning (Denzin, 1991 : 13).

The 'other' stands for inferior human beings such as the blacks, the third world people and the women. The portratyal of women in print and electronic media in general is an object of sex. The androcentric belief is that the female is conscious of her beauty and her body being watched and colonized by male gaze. The artists are to deconstruct this concept of female pleasure by employing the postmodern feminist methods of analysis which "reveal the dominant representation of woman as misrepresentations, the restoration of the past of Women's own self-repressentation, the generation of accurate representation of women and the acknowledgement of the need to represent difference among women" (Hutcheon, 1989 : 141).

Thus, the attaempt is to use the art not merely for another representation but for a critical representation. Secondly, it is the urban elites and media people who decide the contents of Media (TV etc.). The decision is commercialized and consumer-oriented and this is far removed from the rural folks and therefore, media are not playing the role of empowerment rather towads disempowerment.

Therefore, the contents are to be analysed for the betterment of womenfolk avoiding all the pornographic representation of women (Joseph, 1997 : 75-80).

Thirdly, in Indian context, girls are taught to keep their problems within themselves. They are asked not to disclose them before others. Such secrecy breeds many problems and diseases, including mental and psychological imbalances. It is the high time that media should project all the problems to educate women for improving their physical, mental and psychological health. A feminist postmodern cultural studies program is therefore, an uneasy encounter which would seek to avoid essentialist, functional categories and dichotomies public/private, mothering/fathering functions, reproduction biology/culture, fixed gender identites and so on. It would be historically and situationally specific grounded in the particular class, race-gender economic-ideological configurations that operate in a particular time and place. It would posit a multiplicity of subject positions, not just the 'unitary notions of women, or female gender identity, treating gender as one relevant strand among others, attending also to class, race, ethnicity, age and sexual orientation' (Fraser, 1988 : 391). It would study how gender is enlivend through sexuality (Lacan, 1982), as it examines how the master narrative of patriarchy is woven through the reinforcing myth of Eros, Youth, Beauty and Love. It would study how these narratives are implemented in everyday life through a political economy of signs and difference which turn women into commodities, desire into sexuality, and erotic love into pronography (Denzin, 1993 : 18).

Thus, a Feminist, Postmodern Cultuaral Studies moves around how the worlds of patriarchy are lived into existence. How dominant and subordinate sexual codes (homosexual, lesbian, male, female, love, sex, intercourese) are represented, acquired and enacted. The guiding question in such inquiries becomes, how the lived experiences of sexuality depart from, yet articulate and amplify, the mythical beliefs that operate in the popular culture about love, family eroticism and the relations between the sexes.

Conclusion

In Multicultural countries, such as nation, language, race and sex are cultural specific despite their similarity. Gates says that

"Multiculturalism is concerned with representations, not of difference as such, but of cultural identities, while Guiding Howe declares that the critic, the writer and the audience — all are rooted in their biographies and historical circumstances. Art is neither anonymous nor universal : it springs from the particular of gender as well class, race, age and cultural experience. Identity, Theory and Feminie Gender representation are, therefore, a part of Cultural Studies.

The Feminine gender identity however, appears and disappears across the cultures as a part of literary history which is grounded in the experience of deprival and disadvantaged. Showalter argues that there is a universal patterning in the representation of women (images, themes, plot etc.) regardless of socio-economic and political context in which the text are produced. To approach such patterning, she propounds two theories of criticism — the first is women as a reader while the second is concerned with women as a writer. In 1970s it has been realised that feminism itself was no longer necessary since equality of opportunity for women had been achieved. Therefore, the method of postfeminism text analysis emerged in 1980s.

Critics like Linda Hutcheon links feminism with postmodernism. Both worked to help us to understand the dominant modes of representation at work in our society. Feminism has focused on the specifically female subject of representation and has begun to suggest ways of challenging and changing those dominants in both mass culture and high art. They have taught us that to accept unquesioningly any fixed representations — in fiction, film, advertising or whatever — is to condone social system of power which validate and authorise some images of women (or blacks, Asians, gay etc.) and not others. Cultural production is carried on within a social context and an ideology and lived value system — and it is this that feminist-work has made us pay attenition. Feminisms have in this ways, had a very profound effect on post-modernism.

In fact, the Western Feminist movement fought for undeclared sex orientation while the feminist movement in the developing countries is based upon socio-economic issues (such as sati, dowry, rape, violence etc.). However, all agree that there exist a gender-struggle, gender power-politics and its solution lies in empowerment of women rather than emancipation. Reservation for women, legal provisions and Women Welfare Programmes etc., can be suitable strategies for substantial feminine representation in various walks of life. In the Indian context, the movement has divergences between urban and rural upper class and lower (Dalits), class women. However, there is an awakening of new rural based feminist after (1975) which rejected 'Sita-Savitri' ideal challenging religious domination and praising 'Stri-Shakti' and 'Laxmi-Mukti' and rebuliding and self-reliant 'Sita temple' which sumbolizes rehabilitation of Matriarchy over Patriarchy.

Thus, the change in sexual revolution came into two successive waves. The first marched under the banner of freedom and the second under feminism that of equality. Yet European society shows differences in simplistic opposition to each other; dominant/ subordinate, good/bad, up/down, superior/inferior. So the inferior or oppressed group in their society is made of Black, third world people, working class, older people and women who have yet to achieve freedom and equality, therfore, Post-feminist stage is beyound their reach. Since all the readings are not endowed with transcendental (constantive) meanings, the textual meaning for these disadvantaged classes especially for women is searched in their socio-economic and historical condition, which demands a different aesthetics.

REFERENCES

Anderson, Benedict, 1991, *Imagined Communities*, London : Verso.

Bharti, A. 1985, "The Self in Hindu Thought And Action," in *Women and Self*, ed. A.J. Marselas G. Devos, New York : Tavistock Pub. 185-230.

Bhattacharjee, Anannya, 1999, "The Habit of Ex-nomination : Nation, Woman and the Indian Immigrant Bourgeosie," in *Emerging Voices* ed. Sangeeta R. Gupta, New Delhi : Sage Pub.

Das, Gurucharan, 1997, "Cultural Complexes : Modern without becoming Western," *Times of India*, New Delhi, 10th Dec.

Davis, Robert Con. and Rinald Schleifer, 1988, ed. *Contemporary Literacy Criticism* : Literary and Cultural Theory. New York : Longman.

Denzin, Norman K., 1991, *Images of Postmodern Sociey : Social Theory and Contemporary Cinema*. New Delhi : Sage Pub.

Docherty, Thomas, 1933, *Post-Modernism : A Reader*. New York : Harvester.

Eagleton, Mary, 1994, *Feminist Literary Theory*. Cambridge : Blackwell.

Fraser, Nancy and Nocholson Linda, 1988, "Social Criticism without Philosophy : An Encounter between Feminism and Postmodernism," *Theory, Culture and Society*, 5 : 373-94.

Gates Henry Lewis, Jr., "Beyond the Culture Wars : Identities in Dialogue," *Profession,* 93 : 6-11.

Gopal, S., 1993, "On Nationhood, National Identity : A Historical Perspective," a lecture delivered at NIAS, Bangalore on 11th Jan. (Tape Recorder).

Gupta, Sangeeta R., Emerging Voices : *South Asian Woman, Redefine Self, Family and Community*, New Delhi : Sage Publications.

Hutcheon, Linda, 1989, *The Politics of Pastmodernism,* London : Routledge.

Hutcheon. Linda, 1995, "Incredulity towards Metanarrative : Negotiating Postmodemism and Feminism," *Canadian Contexts*. Delhi : Pencrat International.

Joseph, Ammu, 1997, "Electrionic Democracy : An Indian Perspective," *V NIAS Course for University and College Teachers.* Bangalore, 75-80.

Lorde, Andre, 1990, *The US in Modern Age*, ed. Carl Bode. Washington. USIA, 292-95.

Marwah-Roy, A, 1999, "Globalization, Tradition and Indian Women," *Span* VL, 5, Sept./Oct.

Mancken, H.L., 1990, "Feminism Comes of Age in American Perspective," *The US in Modern Age,* ed. Cark Bode. USIA Washington DC.

Patel, Sujata, 1995, "The Ideological and Political Crisis of Early 90's Contradiction in Indian Society," India Munsi, Jaipur Rawat, Pub.

Selden, Raman, 1989, *Practicing Theory and Reading Literature :* An Introduction. Kentucky : The Univ. of Kentucky.

Toffier, Alvin, *Future Shock,* London, Pan Books.

4

Caste Conflict in Mulk Raj Anand's Major Novels

—Mrs. Pradnya V. Ghorpade

SOCIAL inequality is a keynote of the caste system. The superiority of one caste over the other does not necessarily mean domination of one caste over the other. It is more accurate to think of the caste system as constituting a multiplicity of hierarchies determined by custom within various geographical areas of organization. The relationship of one caste to another is not similar to that which exists between master and slave. The inferior-superior relationship of a caste may be stated in terms of its purity. In this context, Ketkar remarks : "A caste is pure or impure according to its hierarchical position."[1] Untouchability is the characteristic fact of Hindu Society. The caste system constitutes the structure of Hinduism as a religion is a system of beliefs and doctrines developed about the basic principle of *Karma.* Caste is the very core of Hindu religion. As M.K. Gandhi observes : "If untouchability was a part of the Hindu creed, I should decline to call myself a Hindu and most decidedly embrace some other faith if it is satisfied my honest aspirations." Gandhi further states, "Fortunately for me, I hold that untouchability is not a part of Hinduism."[2] Caste is such an obtrusive factor of Indian social organization. During the British rule the untouchables were really unapproachable. Gandhi says, "Untouchability means pollution by the touch of certain persons by reason of their birth in a particular state of family."[3] Caste system generates the feeling of 'superiority' or 'inferiority' in the minds of caste-based society. Untouchability is described as a sin, blot, curse and stain imposed on a group of people by another group of people.

I wish to discuss Mulk Raj Anand's major novels in the context of caste conflict in India.

Mulk Raj Anand's major novels like *Untouchable* (1935), *Coolie* (1936), *The Big Heart* (1945) and *The Road* (1961) deal with the miserable lives of the downtrodden and poor outcaste society. All his protagonists belong to different castes/classes, and they are victims of either caste/class conflict or victims of male-dominated social system. K.N. Sinha rightly observes : "These novels, *Untouchable, Coolie, Two Leaves and a Bud, The Big Heart* and *The Road* not only present a mirror reflection of the actual life.... but the catharsis of pity."[4]

The novel *Untouchable*[5] was published in 1935. It presents a set of adolescent characters — Bakha, Rakha, Sohini, Ramcharan, the leather worker's son — Chhota and so on. Bakha is a central character in the novel. Mulk Raj Anand has described various episodes in the life of Bakha during the course of a day. The very location of the colony is a segregated place of the outcastes where Bakha was born. In the beginning he is childlike and unresentful by nature. He forgets all insults. He differs also from other sweepers as he is a champion of all games as well as very responsible and conscious. But at the end of the day, he gives up his hope of becoming a gentleman and realizes his true identity in his life.

The novel narrates a series of insults imposed on a young sensitive boy. Bakha is a victim of the present caste and class system. The novel shows that Bakha is representative of the untouchables. But it does not mean that Bakha has not his own identity. E.M. Forster has rightly pointed out : "Bakha is a real individual, lovable, thwarted, sometimes grand, sometimes weak and thoroughly Indian."[6] Bakha's daily work is cleaning latrines as he goes out to sweep the main road and the temple courtyard in the town. The day begins with abuses from his father while awakening him : "Are you up? Get up, you illegally begotten ..."(25). After finishing his morning round, he goes to the town. He passes by the fruit stalls, sweet-meat stall and so on. Once, he bought *jilebis*. He put a piece in the mouth. But then he forgot to announce his arrival. He 'touched' a man, *i.e.*, Lalaji, who hurled vulgar abuses at Bakha and attracted a big crowd around them. Bakha felt sorry and begged forgiveness of Lalaji. But the 'polluted' man slapped him. Bakha's turban fell off and the *jilebis* were scattered in the dust. Then he realized his place and position in the society : "All of them abused. Why are we always abused?... Because we touch dung. It is only the Hindus and the outcastes who are not sweepers for them I am sweeper — Untouchable! Untouchable! That's the world! I'm an Untouchable!"(72).

Later, a caste woman abuses him while offering the food. He tries to have a close look at the God in the temple. But the people shout that he has polluted the temple.

Bakha has a sister named Sohini. As she approaches the well, she has to face the abuses thrown at her by those belonging to the higher castes. Kalinath, the priest is impressed with her attractive attentions and when she comes to clear the courtyard, he makes improper suggestions to her. But on her denial, he starts shouting 'polluted, polluted', and soon several high caste people gather there. Bakha can do no more than rage against the brutalities of the upper castes. After sending his sister home he goes to the silversmith's lane to fetch food. There an orthodox housewife is mad with fury because she feels that Bakha has defiled her house by contact. Later, in the course of a 'hockey game', when a boy is injured, Bakha tries to lift him up. But the boy's mother is angry with him that he is 'polluted'. The religion, the family are not safe places for this young boy. Right from the morning, Bakha suffers a series of insults at the hands of the caste Hindus. Cigarettes are flung at him as a bone is flung at dog, *jilebis* are thrown at him like a cricket ball and the *chapatis* fly down at him from the third floor. Bakha belongs to the lowest of the low caste — the sweeper : "They think we are mere dirt, because we clean their dirt" (99). His identity is : "I am untouchable! An untouchable, posh, posh, sweeper coming!" (109). Bakha's consciousness, his acceptance of his identity is the climax of his inner conflict. Wherever he goes, he is greeted with such words as 'defiled', and 'polluted'. His passiveness in the novel is a burden of tradition.

Bakha's love for modernity is his attempt to protect himself against the evil caste/class system. He wants to wear the sahib's clothes and speak his language. This love for modern English life is his illusion which allows him to forget the reality about him. He heard the public speeches of Mahatma Gandhi : "I regard untouchability as the greatest blot on Hinduism" (157), and the poet, Iqbal Nath Sarshar : "Then the sweepers can be free from the stigma of untouchability and assume the dignity of status that is their right as useful members of a casteless and classless society" (158). Bakha is impressed and feels more hopeful of the future and returns to his house to tell his father about the Mahatma and about the machine that will 'clear dung without anyone having to handle it.' E.M. Forster comments : "It is the necessary climax, and it has mounted up with triple effect. Bakha returns to his father and his wretched bed thinking now of the Mahatma, now of the machine. His Indian day is over and the next day will be like it, but on the surface of the earth if not in the depth of the sky, a change is at hand."[7]

The consciousness of Bakha is totally opposite to the fatalistic approach of his father, Lakha. Lakha's reaction to the Pandit's attempt to molest Sohnini is as follows : "We can't do anything. They are our superiors. One word is sufficient against all that we might say before the police. They are our masters. We must respect them and do as they tell us. Some of them are kind" (87-88).

Mulk Raj Anand published his second novel, *Coolie*[8] in 1936. The novel narrates the life story of a young hill-boy, Munoo. Basically, *Coolie* is a character novel and Munoo is the major character. By caste, he belongs to the second highest caste — Kshatriya in Hindu society. His life in Babu's house is the routine of domestic slavery. His poverty forces him to leave his village. He tries to seek his place and position in society but the society denies him this place. The society gives him only economic insecurity. But Munoo's upper caste gives him free access to all the classes of society.

Coolie is a novel which is an attempt to read beyond caste system and explore the economic implications of the situation. As a result, Anand explores the connection between class and imperialism on the one hand, and on the other he suggests a complicated motif of caste/communal conflict interrelated to imperialism and capitalism. His preoccupation with caste/class system and poverty and misery is unmistakable.

The Hindu-Muslim communal riot at the meetings of the trade

union leaders is another conflict in the novel. These meetings are disturbed by the rumours that some Hindu children have been kidnapped by pathans. Several are killed, many are wounded in the furious riot. Mulk Raj Anand points out how men become the victims of communal jealousy and religious fury. The communal conflict is an extension of caste conflict. In this manner, both caste conflict or communal conflict and class conflict are interrelated.

Like Bakha, Munoo also uses flow of abusive words like, 'You of the evil start', 'liar', 'vulgar', 'brute', 'stupid', etc. In this novel, the society of coolie is one in which the chief form of exploitation is capitalist. Munoo's experiences are totally different from Bakha's. But on mental level, he, like Bakha, is a passive character. It seems that mere survival is the assertion of personality for these caste and class untouchables. Munoo's upper caste gives him free access to all the classes of society. Munoo is also an 'outcaste', his insignificance in the world is the same as that of the untouchables. He is downtrodden and rejected by everyone because of his 'poverty.' He is an insignificant part, like the millions of workers.

The communal conflict is an extension of caste conflict. In this manner, both caste conflict or communal conflict and class conflict are interrelated. In the Indian situation, this is peculiarly an Indian phenomenon, where the conflicts originate both in traditional orthodox of castes as well as the systematic capitalistic situation obtaining in the urban society. The complications are obvious enough. Anand does not seem to deal with both these conflicts in this novel in a headlong manner, but touches upon it rather superficially. Poverty is the root cause of Munoo's tragedy. His life is severely circumscribed by the adverse circumstances wherever he goes. His own career is varied; almost a domestic slave at Shamnagar, a boy-worker in a pickle factory at Daulatpur, a labourer at the New George Cotton Mill and at last a coolie at Simla. He is exploited all the time by one person or other. As Dr. K.R.S. Iyengar observes : "*Coolie* is varily a cross-section of India, the visible India, the mixture of the inhuman and the human, the sordid and the beautiful."[9]

In *Coolie,* we see that caste monopoly has given place to money values superficially. The foreign exploiters and the masses of the exploited (the coolies) make the main pattern of tension in the novel.

Mulk Raj Anand's next novel *The Big Heart*[10] (1945) focuses on the significant theme of untouchability. To begin with, the story exposes the conflict between sub-castes. Thathiar and Kasera are the sub-castes in the community of the coppersmiths. Ananta, the protagonist is a coppersmith, who belongs to the Thathiar and returns to his home in the Billimaran kucha of Amritsar after having worked in factories in Bombay and Ahmedabad. He brings his beloved Janki, a young widow, with him. In this town, Lalla Murli Dhar and Seth Gokul Chand have established a factory which manufactures war tools. It has created a peculiar unrest. Many thathiars have been rendered jobless because of the introduction of the machine. Ananta tries to gather all the jobless coppersmiths into a union. So that they can demand their jobs and justice from the factory owners, the capitalists.

The caste and class conflicts are finely interrelated to each other in the novel. Anand exposes the interpersonal relations among the high castes. Kasera and Thathiar are sub-castes of the Kshatriya coppersmith community. Kaseras suppose themselves superior to the Thathiars; and they would be polluted by contact with the sub-caste. They believe in a legend. "To Ram was given an arrow, to Sita bow, and from them the truly nobel order of Kshatriya Kaseras is descended" (129). This deep-rooted caste-consciousness is revealed by Mulk Raj Anand. As Saros Cowasjee points out : "*Untouchable* dealt primarily with the caste problem and *Coolie* with the class problem. *The Big Heart* touches on both these problems, showing how they react on each other!"[11] The Thathiars never want to revolt against their caste exploitation. The cruelty of the Kaseras is unnecessary. The thathiars endlessly suffer at the hands of the rich Kaseras. Ananta is conscious of it, as he says : "... we suffer from the day we are born till the day we die; but this cruelty is unnecessary. A little reason could settle this difficulty between the Kaseras and us" (136). Mulk Raj Anand has described the two groups of these two sub-castes in the following words : "... the beautiful copper, brass, silver & bronze utensils made in the lane are sold by dealers called Kaseras ... In the new Iron Monger's bazar ... there are the screws and bolts and nails and locks are sold by thathiars..." (8).

The thathiars are lower because they work with their hands. As Anand points out : "... the thathiars are craftsmen, doing dirty, grimy, ill-paid work with their hands, had come to acquire a low professional status in Hindu society" (127).

Gokul Chand is a Kasera and the Choudhari of utensil seller's community. Lala Murli Dhar is a thathiar and the leading person in the coppersmith brotherhood. They establish a factory manufacturing war tools. Their relations are based on cash nexus. They are partners, but their friendship seems to be stained because of caste differences. Anand has tried to project the interaction of the two evils — class and caste in *The Big Heart*. As M.K. Naik observes : "In Billimaran ... the worst in old tradition joins hand with the worst in modern capitalism in an unholy alliance of forces of exploitation"[12] The caste and class conflict in the novel is not as dominant as in Anand's earlier novels. But *The Big Heart* dwells on an aspect of casteism that has not received any serious attention.

Mulk Raj Anand's next novel *The Road*[13] which was published in 1961, deals the theme of untouchability. In this novel, Bhiku, the protagonist is a road-worker. Bhiku's condition is no different from Bakha's condition. Bhiku is very defiant by nature. Caste is the chief target of Anand's criticism in *The Road*. In this novel we find that, caste-consciousness on the part of the orthodox Hindus results in an number of obstacles in the path of the progress of the poor out-castes of the village. In addition to it Rama Jha's comment is : "Anand takes up more directly both the theme and character the Untouchable once again in the context of politically free India."[14] Anand's humanistic approach is echoed by B. Gupta as he says : "*The Road* re-affirms Anand's inalienable faith in the essential dignity of man, whatever be his caste and position in society."[15]

A group of outcastes is working to build the road under the leadership of a sympathetic Caste-Hindu in the village Govardhan. The road will help them to transport milk to the nearby towns easily. But some higher castes men refused to touch these 'polluted' stones handled by the outcaste labour. The landlord Thakur Singh is jealous of the untouchable for the reason that they have now started earning wages. So he tries to prevent them from their earnings in various ways. But the untouchables are not frightened by Singh's cunning plans; instead they successfully complete the building of the road with the help of the Government. At the end of the novel, the hero Bhiku, tired by the caste-hatred in the village, moves away along the new road to Delhi, a place where people are too busy and 'no one knew who he was and where would be no caste or out caste' (96). The road to Delhi is to be the road to freedom from caste-hatred.

The untouchables are not allowed to enter into the temple or to walk on the village earth because they are out caste. Bhiku's mother simply says to her son, "We are *Chamars* and they are twice-born" (6). Her traditional mind and timidness shows that caste consciousness is universal and very natural in Hindu society. But Bhiku's rejection of this conventional attitude is a hint of conflicts. He angrily says, "One is a leather worker by profession and not by birth" (6). At the end of the novel, Thakur Singh, the orthodox landlord wishes to meet Bhiku. In Thakur's house Bhiku begs for a glass of water. But Thakur's young son pulls the brass cup out of Bhiku's hand angrily and shouts that the whole house will have to be purified. Bhiku, like his prototype Bakha, for moment thinks of retaliating but he remembers that he is a *Chamar,* untouchable and he controls himself. Bhiku runs to Delhi to escape untouchability. The road here is a symbol of prosperity and progress. The problem here has been treated as a sociological one. In this novel, Anand narrates the story of Bhiku and his *Harijan* friends who build a road for the Government and come in conflict with caste Hindus who do not want to touch the stones defied by the so-called *Chamars*.

In *Untouchable* Bakha returns at the end of the novel to his home with hope for 'change.' In *The Road* Bhiku decides to leave his own village and marches towards the town to escape from the caste-Identity. This may be described as romantic idea, but in reality migration of the untouchables to the city for a better deal is a reality. The novel *The Road* is a new work on the same theme of untouchability, but in a different situation, that is of Independent India. While *Untouchable* is a dramatic presentation of a day's experiences in the life of Bakha, *The Road* is literary romance dealing with various other aspects of untouchability in the changed world.

In short, Mulk Raj Anand deals with the caste conflict in these novels very realistically. The miserable lives of the downtrodden and poor outcaste people is presented there superficially. These novels present a mirror reflection of the actual life and suffering of outcaste people.

REFERENCES

1. S.V. Ketkar : *The History of Caste in India*, Vol. II, New York and London : 1909, p. 23.
2. M.K. Gandhi : *Young India,* 1924-1926, New York, 1927, p. 12.
3. A.T. Hingorani : *My Philosophy of Life,* By M.K. Gandhi, ed., A.T. Hingorani Bombay : Pearl Publication, 1961, p. 146.
4. K.N. Sinha : *Mulk Raj Anand,* Delhi : Kalyani Publishers, 1989, p. 27.
5. M.R. Anand : *Untouchable,* New Delhi : Arnold Heinemann, 1981.
6. E.M. Forster : *Preface to Untouchable,* New Delhi Arnold Heinemann, 1981, p. ii.
7. E.M. Forster : *Preface to Untouchable,* p. vii.
8. M.R. Anand : *Coolie,* New Delhi : Arnold Heinemann, 1981.
9. K.R.S. Iyengar : *Indian Writing in English,* Bombay : Asia Publishing House; 1962, p. 265.
10. M.R. Anand : *The Big Heart,* New Delhi : Arnold Heinemann, 1945.
11. Saros, Cowasjee : *So Many Freedoms,* Madras : Oxford University Press, 1977, p. 127.
12. M.K. Naik : *Mulk Raj Anand,* Delhi : Heinemann India, 1973, p. 80.
13. M.R. Anand : *The Road,* Delhi Sterling Publishers Pvt. Ltd., 1987.
14. Rama, Jha : *Gandhian Thought and Indo-Anglian Novelist,* Delhi Chanakya Publication, 1983, p. 82.
15. Balarama, Gupta : *Mulk Raj Anand,* Bareilly : Prakash Book Depot, 1974, p. 33.

5

The Pattern of the Narrative Voice in Mulk Raj Anand's *Untouchable*

—Dr. V. Thanuvalingam

IN a novel, the narrator, the second self of the author who may otherwise be called the implied author, plays a significant role in evolving the fiction experience of the reader, and this survey aims at an analysis of the narrative techniques of Mulk Raj Anand in his first novel which he published in 1935. The oneness of the experience, the reader gains at the end of his perusal will be determined by the nature of the narrative mode which a writer adopts in a work. In fiction narratology, irrespective of the languages, there are only two modes of narration and they are "telling" a fiction and "showing" it. While "telling" a story, a writer often intrudes in the course of the narrative and supplies information about the fictional material. Wayne C. Booth says that "in literature from the very beginning we have been told motives directly and authoritatively without being forced to rely on those shaky inferences about other men which we cannot avoid in our own lives."[1] In "showing" fiction, the narrator minimizes his presence or interference in the text and allows the reader to experience fiction on his own without much of comments. "Telling" and "showing" are the two major critical canons of Wayane C. Booth and in this paper, they are applied to Anand's *Untouchable* for discovering the nature of his narrative mode.

The narrative voice or the narrator (the two terms are synonymously used) takes omniscience over the fictional material — the characters, events, incidents, episodes etc., — and presents the story. While presenting the story, the narrator keeps a distance from the fictional material, and depending on the situation, the nature of the fictional material and to some extent whims and fancies, he (the narrator) moves close to the fictional material, through overview comments or keeps away from it by being reticent. When the narrative voice moves close to the fictional material it takes unlimited omniscience over it and supplies all information about it in advance. When he keeps a wide distance from the material, the omniscience will be limited and the reader is not supplied much of information about the fictional material.

Mulk Raj Anand, with the zest of a social reformer, in his *Untouchable*, portrays the sufferings and pains of the underdogs in the Indian society, and the narrator here takes a limited and unlimited omniscience over the fictional material on different occasions. It is a story about Bakha, the scavenger and it begins with a description of the outcastes' colony on the outskrits of the Bulandshahr town. The detailed account of the houses, the outcastes living there, the soiled brook, the slushy land, the dirt and filth, and the human refuse in the area evoke a sense of evulsion. At the outset, Bakha is established as the viewpoint character and thus, the writer assumes unlimited omniscience over the principal actor. The author presents the sensibility of Bakha in the opening of the novel :

> And altogether the ramparts of human and animal refuse that lay on the outskirts of this little colony, and the ugliness, the squalor and the misery which lay within it, made it an 'uncongenial' place to live in.
>
> At least so thought Bakha, a young man of eighteen strong and able-bodied, the son of Lakha the Jemadar* of all the sweepers in the town and the cantonment, and officially in charge of the three rows of public latrines which lined the extremest end colony, by the brook-side.[2]

The narrative voice remains close to Bakha, and maintains almost a negligible distance from him. Since the narrative voice

*Head or Foreman.

has started the story from Bakha's viewpoint, the reader, through a habit of expectation, anticipates Bakha to be the viewpoint character. The proximity of the narrator to Bakha confirms his being the viewpoint character. The description of the outcastes' colony is veritable, for the slums in towns and urban cities in India look so, and any reader with a little amount of imagination could visualize Bakha's place.

"We bring to the reading of a book certain imaginative faculties which are in use all the day long, faculties that enable us to complete, in our minds, the people and the scenes which the novelist describes — to give them dimensions, to see round them, to make them real."[3] From the description, it could be understood that the narrative mode presented in the situation is that of "telling."

A novel centres on a conflict which is explicitly or implicitly stated, developed and progressively carried forward till the end through characters in action, there interaction supported by events, situations, milieus and sometimes by authorial comments. In *Untouchable* the conflict is presented in the opening page itself, *viz.*, Bakha craves the life style of the Tommies who treat him "as a human being," and he wants social recognition from others. In developing this conflict, the implied author adopts the two fictive modes, "telling" and "showing."

When Bakha is tired after the day's work, he is hungry and since there is no water at home, Sohini, Bakha's sister, goes to the well to fetch water. The implied author takes omniscience over her and "tells" her feelings. Even while a little away, Sohini is full of "anxiety" to see the crowd at the well because she fears that her chance of getting water might be delayed. But her feelings change soon. It is observed that she is not as much "depressed" as she anticipated because, on arrival at the well, she could see only nine people waiting and hers will be the tenth place. It is "reported" further that Sohini forgets the crowd at the moment and remembers her brother with affection. He was tired and thirsty after scavenging, and she could not prepare tea for him because there was no water at home. When she started from the house to fetch water, she felt like a mother for her children. The implied author "assures" the reader that on remembering her brother, Sohini feels disappointed again. There is no sign of a caste-Hindu passing by the well who could help the crowd pull a few buckets of water from the well (the low-castes were not allowed to draw water from the well in the 1930s and 40s in India). She sits patiently waiting for her change. The narrative voice "tells" the situation :

> She had sensed with her deep woman's instinct the feeling in her brother's soul. He was tired. He was thirsty. She had felt like a mother as she issued from her home to fetch water, a mother going out to fetch food or drink for her loved ones at home. Now as she sat in a row with her fellow-sufferers, her heart sank. There was no possible benefactor. But she was patient. She had in her an instinctive fortitude, obvious in her curious reserve, in her composed and peaceful bearing.[4]

The implied author, on this scene, "directs" the reader how to respond to Sohini's feelings as he desires and therefore he "tells" everything. When Sohini is at a distance from the well, she is "anxious' and the reader is "informed" of it. Similarly when she comes close to the well, the "anxiety" disappears in her face. The implied author, in this manner, "tells" Sohini's fear, disappointment and patience. By "telling" the situation in this way, the narrator judiciously prepares the reader for an understanding of Sohini in a right perspective. Through this "telling", the conflict is developed further.

After cleaning the commodes in the barracks, Bakha arrives at the temple to sweep the front of the shrine. The inside of a Hindu temple, the presence of whatever "force" is there inside the temple, the devotees and their clamour for reaching that "force" have been a mystery all along to Bakha. His "fear," "respect" and curiosity for the sanctum of the temple had hitherto been only a vague sensation, but at this finest moment in the novel, his emotion, central and vital to the novel in this phase, crystalizes. Bakha is excited; the temple's massive stone structure, the carved masonry, the exuberance of the intricate decorations strike "a strange kind of awe into his being." He seems to respond to "some unknown force that seemed to lurk there." Bakha, presented almost like a child of nature, is prepared for a new experience, an experience that he never has imagined. He is agitated and soon calmed by the slate coloured fawn blue pigeons and their cooings. He stands in despair, fear and a sense of longing for a new experience when he hears the "loud soprano of Om Shanti Deva" and the loud notes of the conch. Bakha seems to experience a new reality.

The quiet little shrine of a moment ago had become a feeling reality...

> Bakha was profoundly moved. He was affected by the rhythm of the song. His blood had coursed along the balanced melodic line to the final note of strength with such sheer vigour that his hands joined unconsciously, and his head hung in the worship of the unknown god.[5]

Undoubtedly, this is an excellent moment for Bakha and the reader also becomes a partaker of a solid fiction experience. Bakha is an untouchable and therefore he has not entered the temple so far in his life. For the first time, standing on the threshold of the temple, he sees the deity and the "pooja." The narrator interferes here and "tells" all about the feelings of Bakha which normally the reader would not know and this is a fine example of "telling" fiction.

In the mid-segment of the novel Bakha goes over to the barracks to meet Havildar Charat Singh so as to receive a hockey stick from him. Charat Singh sends Bakha to the barracks-kitchen to get tea for him. Bakha meets the cook and now in this situation, the implied author assumes omniscience over the cook and "tells" his feelings. The cook questions Bakha's identity. Before Bakha could answer, the cook starts guessing about him, and his thoughts are commented upon. He thinks that he has seen Bakha somewhere but could not identify him. He might be a sapper. The narrative voice speaks further through the viewpoint of the cook that sappers are of the caste of grass-cutters who are above outcastes. Since the grass-cutters are touchables, no one would mind sending them errands. Besides, he doubt not about Bakha because he owes money to Charat Singh, the implied author assures. Charat Singh had given him a new shirt and a white turban before he (the cook) proceeded on leave. Therefore the cook does not question Bakha at all. The feelings of the cook are reported :

> The cook looked at Bakha for a moment, as much as to ask : 'Who are you?' He thought he had seen the face somewhere but he couldn't place him. 'He might be one of the sappers,' he concluded charitably, seeing that the man held Havildars Chart Singh's clay basin in his hand. As the sappers, in spite of their dark colour and dirty clothes are of the grass-cutter caste, no one would object to sending one of them on an errand to fetch fire. Besides, the cook was indebted to Havildar Charat Singh. The Havildar had given him a clean, new shirt and white turban before he went on leave.[6]

The narrative voice takes extraordinary "privilege" with even a minor character like the cook and reports all his feelings. Bakha is ill-treated by many others and the cook is one among them. Indeed, the cook does not speak ill of the scavenger but his contempt for him is well commented upon. The reader does not have an opportunity to learn about the cook's views but the implied author, through the technique of "telling," conveys to the reader what transpires in his (the cook's) mind. It is an effective technique which helps the reader in understanding fiction and the character of the cook in a right perspective.

Anand has exploited not only the technique of "telling" but also that of "showing" in this fiction. After drinking tea prepared by his sister Sohini, Bakha goes out to relax with his friends. The friends of Bakha haven't met him since morning and on being asked by them the reason for his absence, Bakha responds to the effect that he has to put in more amount of work for the day, for his father is ill. The friends spend their time in a chit chat and decide on a hockey match. It is a light and gregarious moment in which the narrator does not intervene at all (pp. 53-55). Despite a few chances for intrusion, the implied author "shows" the characters in a jocund mood and the reader experiences fiction on his own. The narrator does not comment on the characters nor does he do on events or episodes or future course of action. It is an unguided fiction experience for the reader and it remains a good example for the technique of "showing" fiction.

Towards the end of the novel, the implied author unfolds the story using the technique of "showing." Mahatma Gandhi addresses a large crowd at the "maidan" situated near the railway station of Bulandshahr town. Gandhiji speaks on the problems of caste, religion and untouchability in India. Caste and untouchability are social evils and they can be eradicated, the Mahatma contends. Bakha attends the meeting but the speech of Gandhi is inapprehensive to him. After the meeting, in the crowd, two persons analyse the speech of Gandhiji : Iqbal Nath, the young poet who edits "Nawan Yug" (New Era) and Mr. R.N. Bashir, Barrister-at-Law. Iqbal Nath is critical of Gandhiji's philosophies. If the "machine" is introduced in India — the flush system — there will not be scavengers and thus untouchability can be eradicated. Bakha is unable to understand the solution to the problem of untouchability as discussed by the two characters. However, he learns vaguely that his problem of handling human refuse will come to an end soon. It is one of the fine fictional moments in the novel which presents a solution to the conflict of the fiction. Caste and untouchability are serious social problems and how to eradicate them is hinted at in this situation. The sensibility of the reader is strong and therefore his response to fiction is quick, and it ficilitates an independent fiction experience within There are no authorial intrusions in the narrative to influence the reader's viewpoint and therefore the aesthetic perception in him assumes a high degree of artistic experience.

The two fiction narrative techniques have thus been exploited in *Untouchable*. While "telling" a story, the author makes frequent intrusions in the narrative and guides the reader's response to fiction. He supplies all information to the reader so as to "tell" him how to appreciate fiction. In "showing" fiction, the author does not interfere at all and allows the reader to experience fiction through the characters' interaction with each other, and exercise of limited omniscience over the fictional material. "The frankly omniscient story-teller has well nigh disappeared from modern fiction."[7] Both the techniques of "telling" and "showing" have their merits and demerits. According to Rimmon-Kenan, "there is nothing inherently good or bad in either telling or showing. Like any other technique, each has its advantages and disadvantages, and their relative success or failure depends on their functionality in the given work."[8] Therefore we cannot say that either of them is better than the other. In general, the nineteenth century British and Continental fiction writers and the writers who had lived before adopted the method of "telling" in their works and the late twentieth century novelists have exploited the mode of "showing" fiction. It is a question of sensibility on the part of a reader in his appreciation of fiction. In historical novels, it is not possible to unfold fiction without "telling". But in social novels, even though the twentieth century critics contend that "showing" is more effective, "telling" may also be adopted depending on the fictional needs. In *Untouchable* Anand has indeed synthesized both "telling" and "showing" and it gives a different fiction experience to the reader.

NOTES

1. Wayne C. Booth, *The Rhetoric of Fiction* (Chicago : Univ. of Chicago Press, 1961), p. 3.
2. Mulk Raj Anand, *Untouchable* (London : Wishart Books Ltd., 1935), pp. 13-14.
3. Percy Lubbock, *The Craft of Fiction* (London : Jonathan Cape, 1965), pp. 8-9.
4. *Untouchable*, pp. 34-35.
5. *Ibid.*, p. 89.
6. *Ibid.*, pp. 158-59.
7. Booth, pp. 40-41.
8. Shlomith Rimmon-Kenan, *Narrative Fiction : Contemporary Poetics* (London : Methuen, 1983), pp. 107-108.

6

Rabindranath Tagore : As a Novelist

—*Hari Om Prasad*

RABINDRANATH Tagore is a celebrated name in the sphere of English literature. His creative genius is so much accounting and his literary output is so much rich and varied that the phrase 'myriad-minded', which Matthew Arnold has used for Shakespeare, can aptly be used for him also. In the realm of Indian English literature he has occupied for himself a very special room of his own class. But those who recognize him as a world-poet alone, who got the prestigious Nobel Prize for literature in 1913, for his immortal poetic work *Gitanjali*, are really doing the same job as we do when we see the seen portion of the iceberg and feel it as its whole. Really Tagore is the fountain source of many literary genres. He is a darling of versatility.

Besides being a great universal poet, the genius of Tagore is also a novelist, dramatist, short-story writer, musician, philosopher, painter, educationist, reformer and critic and in every field he has earned a niche for himself. There is hardly a field of literary activity which is not explored and made fruitful by his daring adventures. His genius enriched whatever it touched. Like the Sun after which he is named, he has shed light and warmth, both on his each choice.

Having wooed and won his Muse, the man in Rabindranath feeling the need of a wider field of activity, of a fuller life, chose to write novels and in a very short period became a novelist of a high order. His novels are so much full of promises and potentialities that they, too, deserve our proper concerns to be evaluated with our proper and critical attention in the light of socio-political culture of the Indian society of the then period.

The setting of his novels is representative and reflective, their characters are natural, realistic, full-blooded and life-like. The socio-religious culture of Bengal during the later half of the nineteenth century is brilliantly portrayed in his novels. Through his novels, he brings out some of the problems of the woman of his age. Different kinds of human relations are portrayed and analysed through the different social-settings. Some of his novels deal with the modern problems of our society and the interest in them centres round the psychological development of characters under the compelling stress of circumstances. Tagore does not adhere to the conventional narrative method, nor does he use the principles of an organic, consequential plot-structure. He also tries through his novels, to focus the attention on some of the bitter truths and cruel customs of the lives and society as well. His novels amuse, perplex and bring out the real literary pleasures. M. Sarada a famous writer, rightly observes :

> "Rabindranath Tagore's contribution to the Indian Novel is 'extraordinary' and 'his place is among the pioneers', Chokher Bali (Binodini) published at the beginning of this century is regarded as the first modern novel of India and established the position of Tagore as the father of the realistic psychological novel. Unfortunately, the contribution of Tagore to the development of the Indian novel has not received from the critics the attention it deserves."[1]

Tagore has written thirteen novels of which nine are translated into English. The translated novels are — *Binodini, The Wreck, Gora, The Home and the World, Chaturanga, Farewell, My Friend, Two Sisters, The Garden* and *Four Chapters*. His four remaining novels which are available in Bengali and not translated into English are -— *Bali Thakuranir Hat, Rajarshi, Prajapatir Nirbandha*, and *Yogayog*.

Binodini (Chokher Bali) is the first important novel by which Tagore's career as a novelist starts. It is in its complex setting, a well-constructed novel, revolving and concentrating on the dilemma of human relationship what takes place behind the staid facade of a well-to-do, middle-class Bengali family of the period. Being the first psychological novel of India, its action centres round the mental conflicts of its all characters. It is truly psychological novel which clearly pictures how passions, savage and violent, are roused within the hearts, seemingly placed, and battles rage until the home is nearly burnt down without flame or smoke being visible to the outside eye. The novel introduces a new trend and has laid out the foundation of a new class of thinking in the modern sense. The main interest of the novel lies in the exploration of the individual personality of its heroine 'Binodini' under her different stages of love and hate. There are only six characters in the novel — a vain and pampered youth, an unheroic hero, the fond mother, devoted and jealous, the simple untutored wife who needed the shock of great sorrow to mature into a woman, the pious aunt who finds refuge in religion, the loyal friend, virtuous and heroic and somewhat of a prig, and the young, beautiful and vivacious widow who gives the name to the English version of the novel. About the novel and the novelist's efforts Krishna Kripalani comments :

> "In no other novel has he watched the human drama with such gentle and calm irony, without the intrusion of poetic rhapsodies or intellectual dissertations. In no other novel has he accepted the kinship between sex and love with such frank sympathy — the white lotus of love rooted in the dark slime of desire."[2]

As the novel is full of dialogues, Masti Venkatesa Iyengar, one of the early critics of Tagore, remarks that it is ".... more like a play than like a novel."

The Wreck (Naukadubi), the second of Tagore's novels to appear in English, is a story based on the dilemma of mistaken identity resulting in an exchange of wives, delightfully told and interspersed with descriptions of nature of extraordinary loveliness. Its interest lies in its romantic episodes and accidents, and not in the development of characters which is neither logical nor realistic. It has to be studied as a purely romantic novel, where everything has to be taken for granted without applying the laws of probability and human psychology. The novel points out how a single accident, the boatwreck of the two marriage parties, plays havoc with the careers of Kamala, Ramesh and Hemnalini, leads to mistaken identities and causes them much mental anguish and turmoil. Here the novelist tries to highlight the problems of the newly emerging educated class and their conflicts with the traditionalists. Further, he focuses on the absurdities and complications that result from the orthodox Hindu, negotiated type of marriages.

Critics are devided on the merit of the novel; some praise it highly while others condemn it, but none can deny its popularity and the fact that the novelist has once again proved his skill in portraying the full-blooded and lively woman characters like Kamala and Hemnalini. Further, it has contributed a lot to the growth of human awareness for the contemporary problems of the society. Krishna Kripalani observes :

> "The popularity of this novel may be gauged from the fact that, with the exception of *Gitanjali*, no other book of Tagore's has been translated into so many languages."[4]

Gora is a remarkable achievement of Tagore's art as a novelist. It is the longest novel of Tagore which has been rightly acclaimed as the greatest novel overwritten in India. It is more than a mere novel; it is the epic type work of India in transition at the most crucially intellectual period of its modern history. No other novel can claim so masterly an analysis of the Bengali intelligentsia of the period, with their divided loyalties, their aspirations and inhibitions, or of the character of Indian nationalism which draws its roots from renascent Hinduism and stretches out its arms towards universal humanism. 'Sukumar Sen' has viewed it as "... Something like Mahabharata of modern India."[5]

'Bhabani Bhattacharya', opines that : "Gora is contemporary and yet timeless" as is the case with many great literary works of the world and "It reaches out towards the universal."[6]

The novel centres around the love theme of the four major characters — Gora — Sucharita and Binoy — Lolita. The most prominent character in the novel is Gora who has an intense love for his country and a hatred for the foreigner. He is both an orthodox Brahmin and an enthusiastic patriot. His attraction and meeting with Sucharita unfold a tie which is stronger than that of tradition; it is more a spiritual attraction which draws them together than the biological attraction which a man feels for a woman. Knowing the secret of his birth when his mind is torn with this conflict vanishes. He is united to Sucharita under the tutelage of the Brahmo Paresh Babu. The portrait of Anandmoyi is an effective conrast to that of Gora. Lolita is lovely, impulsive and restless while Sucharita is calm and quiet. Binoy is a highly educated youth with refinement of manners and culture and his views are liberal and unorthodox. His personality is dominated by that of his friend, Gora. Lolita likes him from the beginning of her first acquaintance with him, but she does not like this weakness in the character of Binoy. These two love stories are utilised by the novelist to reveal the fanatic behaviour of both the Hindus and the Brahmos.

The Home and the World (Ghare Baire) is a great and significant novel. Here the novelist has introduced two themes — the Swadeshi Movement and the extra marital love affair. The first theme has political overtones while the second, exposes the murky morality of high society. Through this "Rabindranath threw a veritable bombshell on the conservative society."[7] The novel depicts, perhaps for the first time in Indian literature a frank analysis of the extra marital love-affair of a woman of society. For this adventurous work the novelist and the novel both had to suffer a lot. 'Krishna Kripalani' describes :

> "The author was accused of being both immoral and unpatriotic. For three long years after its publication the critics continued to tear the novel to pieces — a tribute to its impact on their minds."[8]

Though the setting of the novel is the political excitement in the stormy years in the first decade of the century, the real theme of the novel relates to the responsibilities, trials and adjustments which Nikhil makes in his desire to find his relationship with his wife on truth. The psychological study of relationship between a husband and his wife is the real motive of the novel. The novel relies less on plot than on intimate psychological study of its important character like Nikhil, Bimala and Sandip. As a political social novel, it makes a sharp distinction between two rival impulses — the pure passion for constructive work and the greed and destructive energy.

Among many of the significant factors that have enhanced the quality of the novel is the fact that it has raised certain fundamental issues like the role of women at home and outside, and the equality of the sexes. Apart from these questions of sociological importance, the questions of political importance like the relation between the Hindu and Muslims in a pluralistic society have also been discussed here. Again, the novel is important as it reveals Tagore's views on important political and social issues of the time.

Chaturanga is a fine testament of the sanest and soundest common sense. 'S.C. Sengupta' proclaims that "It rivals the English Gitanjali and Bengali Balaka."[9] It is a novel with a compact and well-nit plot embedded with music and poetry. Though the novel has only four chapters and four characters, one of whom tells the story, it is one of Tagore's best and has been described by a competent critic as 'a work of art without blemish". Here, too, there is a love triangle, one woman and two men. But the theme of love is subordinated to the spiritual quest of the protagonist. Sachis is the central character of the novel. Sribilas is Sachis's friend who marries Damini in the strange circumstance and who narrates the whole story. The part played by Damini as a whole and the portrait of her character has to be studied in the light of Sachis' quest for Truth, the central theme of the novel. In the novel Tagore exposes the religious fanatics who, in the name of Hindu orthodoxy and Vaishnavism, indulge in religious aberrations and self-exhibitionism and mislead the people from the true path of spirituality. Here the conflict is between love and religion, rather spiritual *versus* sensual. 'Niharranjan Ray' praises the novel in these words :

> "One of the finest, one of the tensest and one of the most compact and competent works of art that Tagore ever produced."[10]

Farewell, My Friend (Sesher Kavita) is unique among the

novels of Tagore. In this work, the poet in him once again dominates over the novelist. It is a "great love poem written in prose." It combines lyricism and fiction. 'S.K. Banerjee' is of the opinion that the novel is written in a "more consistent poetic strain and on a more purely poetic theme than perhaps any other novel in the world's history."[11] The novel is popular among the sophisticated and well-read readers and has won generous praise from many mature critics. Exposition and development of love in the heart of four characters — Amit Rai, Labanya, Sobhanlal and Ketaki — is portrayed in this novel. In this testament of love and beauty, the love story of this novel revolves round Labanya and Amit Rai, an affluent Oxford-educated briefless barrister of Calcutta. The characters of Sobhanlal and Ketaki help in the development of the slight story content. The main interest of the story lies in the psychological transformations that take place in Labanya and Amit as a result of their love entanglement. The action of the story begins with a motor collision when Amit's car dashes against Labanya's. This chance collision soon develops into friendship and love. The story takes a sudden turn when Ketaki, Amit's earlier hertthrob arrives in Shillong. The story ends abruptly. Amit marries Ketaki. Labanya decides to marry Sobhanlal and informs Amit about this. The novel is no doubt witty and entertaining but it has also a core of serious purpose which lifts it high above the level of romantic comedy. 'Krishna Kripalani' evaluates this novel in these words :

> "Its modern setting, its playful mocking tone, its challenging style, the author's trick of introducing himself as the butt of the hero's merciless criticism, the scintillating wit of the dialogue and the final tragic note voiced in the beautiful poem at the end which gives the book its title — all these won for the novel an immediate popularity with the young readers."[12]

Two Sisters (Dui Bon) is a simple and short novel, dealing with the usual triangle — two sisters in love with the same man. Here Tagore once again takes up the theme of illicit love as in his other novels. It exposes the problem of psychological maladustment in married life. In this novel Tagore takes up the eternal problem of love and suggests the time-worn solution. In none of his works does Tagore present this tragic problem with as much intensity as he does in this novel. The two sisters — Sarmila and Urmimala stand for the two different aspects of womanhood, the "mother-kind", and the "beloved-kind" Here the novelist wants to clear that no doubt everyman seeks in woman both the kinds but a combination of these two aspects in one woman is an unattainable ideal. So one must make peace with the got kind otherwise the pleasure of married-life will be spoilt, making the two lives miserable, unhappy and wretched. 'Bhabani Bhattacharya' remarks that though the novel may not be comparable to Tagore's best yet it is " a work of art exquisite in its own individual fashion."[13]

The Garden (Malancha) is shorter in length but more dramatic in situation. It is mostly in dialogue. Here we find a sharp study of love and jealousy. The theme is almost similar to that of the previous novel 'Two Sisters', two women and a man, though the rival in this case is not the wife's sister, but the husband's distant cousin. The psychological interest of this novel is, however, of a different nature. The story of this novel is about the illicit love-affair of a middle-aged husband with his sincere and frank cousin. The immoral relation leads a great disaster in the family-relation of Niraja and Aditya who once were the objects of jealousy for their harmony and love. A great transformation takes place after a happy married life for ten years when the wife, Nirja falls ill and to attend on her when her doting husband brings Sarala, a distant cousin with whom he has spent his childhood and youth. The dormant love between Sarala and Aditya is enflamed by Niraja's jealousy and the sweet home is burnt in the passions of hatred and unjustified love. Nirja is the only tragic character portrayed by Tagore with whom he shares no mercy and sympathy. Sarala is the only woman character of Tagore who remains unmarried till the age of thirty-one and goes to prison in the freedom movement of the country, wearing a khadi saree. She is marked by the spirit of self-abnegation. Her character is drawn by Tagore to serve as a foil to Niraja. The novel ends with the ghastly and horrible death of Niraja. It is true as 'Niharranjan Ray' remarks :

"In 'Dui Bon' (Two sisters) the author's sympathy for Sarmila is clear and unmistakable but for Niraja in 'Malencha' (The Garden) he seems to have none; she attracts no love; no admiration, even no sympathy."[14]

Four Chapters (Char Adhyay) Tagore's last novel deals with human values and political ideals. This is the tragic novel of frustrated idealism which is expressed in the language of great vigour and beauty. Though the novel is short, its theme and the background have made it more powerful and interesting. The novel has aroused a great storm of controversy since the political background of the story and the author was mercilessly reviled. The form of the novel is dramatic. The unfulfilled but the passionate love between Ela and Atindra is narrated in all four chapters and the four chapters appears like four acts in a play and dialogues have found their suitable places in it. It is embued with the soul of lyricism also. The novel ends with the sound of a whistle indicating that the police have raided the hideout of the terrorists. In the final scene of the novel, on learning that Atin is to kill her, Ela lays bare her passionate love for him and says in her memorable words :

> "Am I not yours, wholly yours, even in death? Take me. Don't let their unclean hands touch my body, for this body belongs to you."[15]

The heroine of the novel 'Ela' has been supposed as the bravest of all the heroines drawn by the author. He has uttered too many home truths of his time in the novel. 'K.R. Srinivasa Iyengar' tells about the novel :

> "Four Chapters is Tagore's Doctor Zhivago — no more than a miniature, no more than a seed, yet the seed of a mighty banyan."[16]

Taking a square view of things we can safely say that Tagore is a novelist of outstanding calibre. We can say sincerely that though the author is famous as a poet, yet the imprints of his genius cannot be denied in his novels too. His novels are modern in thought and technique. They are very impressive in both theme and technique. In his social novels, different kinds of human relations are beautifully portrayed and the biological relations between man and woman from various angles are taken into account.

Dr. Harish Raizda rightly examines Tagore's novels in his own critical framework and says :

> "The best and the most tangible expression of Tagore's humanism is to be found in his novels. Though nearly each of his novels overflows with the profound love for earth and humanity, it is especially in his four novels — *Gora, Chaturanga* (Broken Ties) *Ghare Baire* (The Home and the World) and *Char Adhyaya* (Four Chapters) that he devises intellectual discussions and convincing situations for asserting the importance of man above all pseudo-religious traditions and narrow-minded sectarianism and nationalism."[17]

NOTES AND REFERENCES

1. M. Sarada : Rabindranath Tagore : *A Study of Women Characters in His Novels*, Sterling Publishers Private Ltd., L-10, Green Park Extension, New Delhi-110016, 1988 (preface).
2. Krishna Kripalani : Rabindranath Tagore : *A Biography*, Visva-Bharati, Calcutta, 1980, p. 194.
3. Masti Venkateśa Iyengar, Rabindranath Tagore, Bangalore : Jeevan Karyalaya, 1946, p. 92.
4. Krishna Kripalani : Rabindranath Tagore : *A Biography*, p. 205.
5. Sukumar Sen, *History of Bengali Literatures*, New Delhi : Sahitya Akademi, 1960, p. 313.
6. Bhabani, Bhattacharya, "*Tagore as a Novelist*," in Rabindranath Tagore, A Centenary Volume, 1861-1961, New Delhi : Sahitya Akademi, 1961, p. 97.
7. Bimanbehari Majumdar, *Heroines of Tagore*, Calcutta : Firma, K.L. Mukhopadhyaya, 1968, p. 246.
8. Krishna Kripalani : Rabindranath Tagore : *A Biography*, p. 263.
9. S.C. Sengupta, *The Great Sentinel*, Calcutta : A Mukherjee and Co., 1948, p. 212.
10. Niharranjan Ray, *An Artist in Life*, Trivandrum : University of Kerala, 1967, p. 232.
11. Professor S.K. Banerjee, Quoted in Krishna Kripalani : Rabindranath Tagore — *A Biography*, p. 352.
12. Krishna Kripalani : Rabindranath Tagore : *A Biography*, p. 351.
13. Bhabani Bhattacharya, "*Tagore as a Novelist*," in Rabindranath Tagore, A Centenary Volume, ed. by S. Radhakrishnan, New Delhi : Sahitya Akademi, 1961, p. 101.

14. Niharranjan Ray., *An Artist in Life*, Trivandrum : University of Kerala, 1967, p. 284.

15. Rabindranath Tagore, *Four Chapters*, Transl., Surendranath Tagore, Visva-Bharati, Calcutta, 1961, p. 8.

16. K.R. Srinivasa Iyengar : *Indian Writing in English*, Sterling Publishers Pvt. Ltd., L-10, Green Park Extension, New Delhi-110016., 1994, p. 110.

17. Dr. Harish Raizada, *Humanism in the Novels of Rabindranath Tagore*, taken from T.R. Sharma (edited) *Perspectives on Rabindranath Tagore*, Indo-English Writers Series, Vimal Prakashan, Ghaziabad-201001, 1986, p. 64.

7

Fertility Symbol in Kamala Markandaya's *Nectar in a Sieve*

—*S.G. Bhanegaonkar*

AS far as the theme of fertility is concerned, the analysis of Kamala Markandaya's *Nectar in a Sieve* has so long remained barren. The immense productivity of Mother Nature, the fruitfulness of trees, the melodious singing of birds, and the blossoming of flowers appear to be Kamala Markandaya's principal concerns in *Nectar in a Sieve;* but it is distressing to know that very little critical attention has been paid to the novelist's major obsessions, of course, except a few passing references. It is deeply shocking to know that Kamala Markandaya's love of nature has so long gone unappreciated, her criticism of industrialization and urbanization has still remained uninterpreted, and her serious obsession with fertility motif has remained without a diagnosis. Today, most of the literary critics in India are busy analysing works of art from the feminist point of view, thereby, knowingly or unknowingly, turning a blind eye to the immediate and major concerns closer to the hearts of creative writers. All of Kamala Markandaya's novels can also be studied in the modern feminist perspective; but *Nectar in a Sieve* is a starting exception in the sense that it is a novel in which Markandaya celebrates, and very much the disappointment of our feminist experts, the basic virtues of traditional Indian women — love for husband and children, a sense of sacrifice for the betterment of family, and delight in fertility. These are the qualities modern women seem to have little regard for, and therefore, are the hearts of such women devoid of simple pleasures of life to which Rukumini, the principal character in *Nectar in a Sieve,* has to face. In *Nectar in a Sieve,* Kamala Markandaya has succeeded in pointing out the natural superiority of Nature over man : it is both an appreciation of Mother Nature's enormous productivity and a çriticism of "the mighty impotence of our human endeavour,"[1] Kamala Markandaya's beautiful descriptions of harvests and her brilliant analysis of motherhood, an indispensable part of womanhood, make *Nectar in a Sieve* a lively and fruitful study in fertility.

Marriage is a symbol of joy, fertility, peace, happiness and above all, hope. It opens up the promises of a brand new future and the first chapter of *Nectar in a Sieve* is devoted to the description of the marriage ceremony of Rukumini's three sisters — Shanta, Padmini, and Thangam. Rukhmini, the youngest of the four sisters, also fantasizes "a grand wedding" for herself "such that everybody will remember when all else is a dream forgotten" (p. 08). A large portion of the novel concentrates on marriages and marital life of major characters, thereby, focusing on the importance of fertility. The Indian society, and especially the rural communities, places a great deal of emphasis on women's productivity. Kamala Markandaya's *Nectar in a Sieve* also focuses on the priorities of rural India which include the productivity of Nature and fertility of women. Rukumini is married off to "a tenant farmer who was poor in everything but in love and care" (08) for his wife, Rukumini. Nathan, Rukumini's husband, was himself "the son of a landless man, had inherited nothing"(p. 136). In *Nectar in a Sieve,* Kamala Markandaya skillfully balances women's fertility with men's futility. Nathan's being landless is a sign of his inherent unproductive characteristic, and he has to depend upon Rukumini's feminine generosity for verifying his manliness.

After her marriage to Nathan, Rukumini sets out to her new-found world, and on their way to Nathan's village, they find that everything in nature is happy with their marriage. Everything in Nature appears to celebrates Rukumini's wedding. The novelists puts it this way :

> We rested a half-hour before resuming our journey. The animals, refreshed, began stepping jauntily again, tossing their heads and jangling the bells that hung from their red-painted horns. The air was full of the

> sound of bells, and of birds, sparrows and bulbuls mainly, and sometimes the cry of an eagle, but when we passed a grove, green and leafy, I could hear mynass and parrots. It was very warm, and, unused to so long a jolting, I fell asleep (p. 09).

It is the freshness, beauty and warmth of Nature and the melodious singing of birds that fill Rukumini's heart with joy and contentment and lull her to sleep.

Nectar in a Sieve celebrates and glorifies the enormous creative capacity of Nature. The novel is replete with words from agriculture such as irrigation, reaping, sowing, ripening, grain, rain, granary, paddy, brook, harvest, fields, soil, earth, well, dams, clay, brook, sunshine, threshing, winnowing, etc. This endless list of words showing Nature's fecundity is an indication of Kamala Markandaya's basic concerns *in Nectar in a Sieve.* Kali and Janaki, Rukumin's new friends, teach her "how to milk the goat, how to plant seed, how to churn butter from milk, and how to mull rice" (p.14). Very soon Rukuraini gets accustomed to a life of hardship and suffering-, but she bears everything with a smiling face, without tears in her eyes, or feeling of melancholy in voice.

Rukumini spends most of her time tending her small garden : the beans, the brinjals, the chilies, and the pumpkins all grow well under her hands and Rukumini's husband Nathan is full of appreciation for whatever little success Rukumini has achieved. In chapter I itself follows Kamala Markandaya's one of brilliant descriptions of Nature's vigorous and vast productivity :

> The soil here was rich, never having yielded before, and loose so that it did not require much digging. The seeds sprouted quickly, sending up delicate green shoots that I kept carefully watered, going several times to the well nearby for the purpose, soon they were not delicate but sprawling vigorously over the earth, and pumpkins began to form, which fattening and soil and sun and water, swelled daily larger and larger and ripened to yellow and red, until at last they were ready to eat (p. 14).

Mother earth is so kind that Rukumini just tickles her with a hoe and she laughs with a harvest. The sprouting of seeds fills Rukumini's hearts with a special kind of joy and excitement. It is the Nature's generosity which brings peace to Nathan's mind and contentment to Rukumini's heart. Rukumini is happy in her small garden and so sincerely dedicated to her work that she feels physically healthy and perfect and spiritually uplifted. Rukumini is satisfied to comprehend the very secret of her life that "the sowing of seed disciplines the body and the sprouting of the seed uplifts the spirit, but there is nothing to equal the rich satisfaction of a gathered harvest" (p. 107). Whenever there is a bumper harvest, Nathan and Rukumini receive the blessings of Nature with great excitement, joy and thankfulness. A good harvest is the confirmation of Nature's fertility and fulfilment of man's desires, it also stands for a fresh new beginning. Though Nathan is poor, he is the happiest man and thinks positively that "I am happy because life is good and the children are good, and you [Ruku] are the best of all" (p. 61). The company of nature is a constant source of joy and wonder for them and in the field, in the grain which has not yet begun to form "lay our future and our hope" (p. 83). Suffering, hardship, and poverty become an inseparable part of Rukumini's life, but she never loses her faith in life, in God, and in herself, because "while there was land there was hope" (p. 136).

The vast productivity of soil is counter-balanced by women's strong desire for fertility. *In Nectar in Sieve*, Kamala Markandaya shows the deepest and most beautiful aspect of women's psyche — *i.e.*, delight in the pangs of pregnancy. Kunti, Rukumini's friend and neighbour, moves gracefully despite her burden. The carefully slow, sensuous, and graceful movement of her hips shows a deep sense of pride and delight which all women claim in being pregnant. Bearing children is not merely a part of women's sexual life, nor it is the result of wild sexual passions" but it is the very essence of womanhood and perfection. It is not surprising to find that, all female characters in this novel long for this most desirable virtue. When Rukmini fails to bear children after her marriage to Nathan, her mother places in her hand "a small stone lingam, symbol of fertility" (p. 22). She even goes secretly to Kenny, an English doctor, for medical treatment and affectionately calls him "my lord, my benefactor" (p. 35). After waiting for 7-8 years for a male child, Rukumini loses her patience and in her speeches she reveals the plight and helplessness of a barren woman who is discarded and looked down upon —

> what have we done that we must be punished? Am I not clean and healthy? Have I not borne a girl so fair, people turn to gaze when she passes? (p. 24).

When Rukumini's desire for male children is granted, she takes great pride in becoming the mother of five healthy sons, who are born one after another with slightest possible gap of time. Rukumini feels as if "all the pent up desires of my childless days were bearing fruit" (p. 26). When Nathan tells Kenny that he is a poor man, Kenny replies Nathan that the father of five healthy sons cannot be poor and his wife, Rukumini, does him a credit.

Delight in motherhood indicates women's quest for perfection; and a woman without a child is 'a failure.' The very existence of women largely relies upon their creative achievements and a woman who is barren is tormented and tortured by her own anxieties and fertility failures. While female characters in the novel represent fecundity, almost all males stand for sterility. Kunti's husband is described as "Slow, sturdy, dependable, rather like an ox" (p. 86), and Ira's husband, himself barren, brings Ira back to her parents and accuses them of cheating him, "You gave me your daughter in marriage, I have brought her back to you. She is a barren women" (p. 54). Had Ira been barren, how could she have conceived when she picks up prostitution not as a means of livelihood, but as a way to fulfil her desire for motherhood. Ira is named after one of the greatest rivers of Asia and "for all things water was most precious to us" (p. 20). Water is a great nurturer and destroyer of human life, and Ira is as pure and powerful as water. Ira destroys her husband as he himself is barren and doesn't understand the purity of Ira's soul, but she looks after her small brothers and old parents, thus, plays the role of nurturer. Ira was married in the month of June which is "the propitious season for weddings" (p. 43) and her child Sacrabani is baptized in spite of his mysterious origin. The naming ceremony of Sacrabani, the bastard, shows that every birth is Nature's gift, an occasion for celebration, a thing of joy and beauty.

In this novel, Kamala Markandaya has placed nature's fertility in sharp contrast with the futility of human endeavours and has attempted to point out the superiority of Nature over man. As the novel concentrates on the suffering of Rukumini and Nathani at the hands of rapid Industrial growth, the fertility symbol, which is dominant in the beginning, becomes dimmer and dimmer. The coming of tannery is a part of the process of industrialization and urbanization; and in this novel it is used to show the futility of artificial growth which suffocates Rukumini and Nathan to death. The tannery represents artificiality and unnaturalness of life and it points out all the evils that money brings. The tannery women remain indoors whereas Rukumini is used "to open fields and the sky and the unfettered sight of the sun" (p. 52). The tannery symbol is used to show the disastrous consequences of industrialization upon rural civilization that regards Mother Nature above everything, even God. Kamala Markandaya views industrialization as a horrible machine that crushes down the lives of innocent, nature-loving people like Nathan and Rukumini. The tannery fails to fascinate Rukumini precisely because it "all is shouting and disturbance and crowds wherever you go, even the birds have forgotten to sing, or else their calls are lost to us" (p. 33). The tannery eventually proves to be Rukumini's undoing : Ira ruins herself at the hands of the throngs that the tannery attracts, Rukumini's sons go to work in a tea plantation in the island of Ceylon because the tannery frowns on them, and the entire family is destroyed by its ruthlessness, and finally, Rukumini and Nathan are forced to leave the village. During their short stay in a city where Rukumini's son lives, Nathan and Rukumini take up to odd jobs like cutting stones, it shows the dry, unpleasant, hard, and monotonous life of city, which ultimately swallows up Nathan. Nathan and his wife desire to go back to the simple pleasures of rural life and their "distaste for the city grew and grew and became a sweeping, pervading hatred" (p. 168). Rukumini's short visit to city only helps to disappoint her, it robs Rukumini of everything, including her husband, Nathan, The city life indicates the impotency of human endeavours and Rukumini soon realizes that "there is a limit to the achievements of human courage" (p. 178). Rukumini goes back to her village after Nathan's death. The very sight of the land creates emotional turmoil in Rukumini's heart and she weeps for joy. It is Rukumini's faith in the fertility of Nature that brings her back to the normal and natural life. The city only complicates human life whereas the jocund company of nature makes life easy, pleasurable, spiritually rewarding, and emotionally soothing. Rukumini cries :

> So good to be home at last, at last, the cart jolted to a standstill. I looked about me at the land and it was life to my starving spirit. I felt the earth beneath my feet and wept for happiness (p. 188).

Kamala Markandaya's *Nectar in a Sieve* extols the jubilant Mother Nature for all her wonderful creative achievements. Fertility is the finest of all qualities that Nature and women are endowed with. It is the only virtue that keeps the cycle of life moving whereas all else is a dream. It is through this gift of fertility that women like Rukumini triumph over the failures and dangers involved in livirig the life. Fertility is the most coveted of all gifts of Nature precisely because it only leads Rukumini towards the life of bliss, perfection, and ecstasy. Fertility is the first and foremost desire of an emotionally wise and mature woman, and Rukumini shows deep wisdom by placing her confidence and faith in motherhood and in nature's enormous productivity. In a nutshell, *Nectar in a Sieve* is the realization of Kamala Markandaya's faith in fertility.

REFERENCE

1. Markandaya, Kamala, *Nectar in a Sieve* (The New American Library : New York, 1954), p. 46. (All subsequent references to the text are from this edition.)

8

Ironic Vision and Social Realism in the Novels of Ruth Prawer Jhabvala

—Arjun Kumar

IN the galaxy of Indian women writing Ruth Prawer Jhabvala has already carved a niche for herself. She has a striking penchant towards Indian life and literature and she exploits it for the growth of her personality. She knows amply that India is "very strong and often proves too strong for European nerves," what Kamala Markandya terms "Undilute East" in Possession — and she also knows that "she is irritable and has ... weak nerves." If it is so, in her novel *A Backward Place* (1965), Judy should be an idealised version of her own type living in India who despite her keen sensibility, reasoned equanimity and poise, is a bit too romantic about material possessions and comforts. Since she has introspected and examined Indians closely, she has acquired an intimate understanding of their ideas, ideals and various modes of life.

Ruth Prawer Jhabvala is a true cosmopolitan — in spite of weak nerves — she views the cultural clash of the East and the West with unprejudiced eyes. Raji Narsimhan has a different feeling :

"She writes about India, of course. But that it is a foreigner's perspective and the voice has unmistakable foreign inflexions have come to be overlooked in misplaced magnanimity towards Indo-English."[1] But her vision is honestly speaking ironic, her major artistic intent being depiction of the gap between human hopes and their means. Therefore, frustration, foibles and absurdities of that middle class life which she has assimilated constitute integrity and centrality of her fiction. Their ironies emanate from constant clash between the real and the romantic, the mundane and the mystical, and the existential and spiritual pre-occupations. This has been the very characteristic feature of all her novels so far : *To Whom She Will* (1955), *The Nature of Passion* (1956), *Esmond in India* (1958), *The Householder* (1960), *Get Ready for Battle* (1962), *A Backward Place* (1965), *A New Dominion* (1973) and *Heat and Dust* (1975).

She has involved herself with the comedy of manners and the weaknesses, absurdities and incongruities of interpersonal relationships. Besides, Mrs. Jhabvala, being an outsider, has studied the characteristic Indian traits from the viewpoint of a culturally advanced on-looker. This expresses partly why she feels sometimes so terribly upset about social manners and even the postulates of Indian life.

Thematically, the pertinent concerns of Mrs. Jhabvala are manners of white-collared people who experience mental agony in their pursuit of modernism as it involves alienation from their familial and cultural roots. She focuses incongruities for intensifying awareness, and not for attacking or providing carping criticism of Indian mode of life, or even for creating ideological statement. Ironies are exposed mainly on three levels — either the incomparability of personal ideal and circumstantial reality : or incongruities consequent upon the inharmonious blending of two modes of life, the Eastern and the Western; or the clash between tradition and modernity within framework of family. Whenever the novelist finds man experiencing discomfiture or behaving in an old way, her comic genius finds itself in readiness to pounce on him. Although usually she takes within her purview the ironies of situation and character and she tries to develop the ironies of incongruous moments quite competently, it is seldom that her total attitude towards life is ironical. Meena Belliappa in *Banasthali Patrika : A Study of Jhabvala Fiction* observes : "Cosmic and existential ironies do not form a part of her plot construction. Her method is to present certain situations and follow faithfully the train of a character in all his thought and feeling creating for the time being an illusion of complete sympathy and endorsement, and to mention just the opposite of that situation to administer them the shock of disillusionment."[2] She possesses a peculiar knack of juxtaposing the two styles of life which at once makes the difference clear. Jhabvala is at her best when she observes acutely oddities of behaviour and response and brings out with gentle irony and good-humoured satire, the comedy of what she observes. Her art, however, suffers when she offers instead well-worn types and stock reactions, when her irony turns arid and her satire borders on cynicism and when she occasionally tries unsuccessfully to plunge into the deeper waters of serious emotional complications.

Structurally, the phenomenal characteristic of her novels is the subtlety and adroitness with which she unravels the gossamer threads of intricate human relationship — especially among the females in the Hindu joint family. She recreates appreciably this drama of cattiness in which conversation is often a veiled battle of polite affronts, the favourit weapons being innuendoes and insinuations, left handed compliments and deadly insults masked as innocuous generalities, while a chance word is a bomb dropped with devilish accuracy and devastating effect. In these battles, old scores are settled and new wounds inflicted, all over a pleasant cup of tea or a glass of sherbet. She observes life with amusement, yet disinterestness is conspicuous by its presence and she underlines what is bizzare, what is knotted with self deception and contradiction, what is ludicrous, what is fantastic, and occasionally — very occasionally — even what is perilously close to tragedy. Jane Austen the great Victorian Novelist works wonder in her little bit of ivory, hardly two inches wide. Jhabvala's is a static society : at least it is recognisably a 'society.'

In Jhabvala's first novel *To Whom She will*, the heroine Amrita is sentimental and intellectually equipped with understanding of her circumstances in spite of her education like Shakuntala of *Esmond in India* (1958). Krishna, Amrita's paying guest who is the best person available for her, but she is absolutely unable to assess his qualities. He has received his education in England. He is gentle, humorous, sober and co-operative. The irony becomes more poignant when she uses him as a tool to hook her lover Hari and Hari himself shows that he loves Amrita, ultimately agrees to marry the girl chosen by his own parents and comes to realise that his wedded spouse is more beautiful than Amrita. Similarly Amrita's love and affection is superficial for Hari. When Hari settles down with the girl, she also, in her desperation, magnifies the importance of Krishna's letter sent from Calcutta and thinks that she has found her anchor. She pours her heart on him. Ironically enough, Krishna is considered to be the best match because "he is a Bengali and later it is discovered that his father has shared a prison sentence with Nirad Chakravarty (her father) in Meerut Jail during 1933-35 : this makes Krishna quite one of the family."[3(text)]

Thus the novel begins with an emancipated heroine's search for proper partner but ends with her gloating on the least attractive proposal. The title of the novel, *To Whom She Will* is extracted from one of the stories of the *panchtantra* where it is mentioned how a girl of tender age chooses to marry on her own the man she loves. In the modern age, history has done to make emancipation a bright achievement, the modern counterpart of the Panchtantra girl, has a timid heart and a fickle mind. Nimmi in *the Nature of Passion*, Shakuntala in *Esmond in India* (1958) and Gulab in *A Backward Place* are all emancipated women, but in their own ways they are versions of the medieval women for their dependence on the security provided by the well knit family. This ironical situation is counterbalanced by the novelist's equally frank portrayal of the European woman — like Betty in *Esmond in India* (1958) and Etta in *A Backward Place* (1965) — whose vision fails to transcend carnal pleasure. Jhabvala's postulates being deep understanding and progressive attitude for any harmonious living together in the modern context, it is conceivable that she highlights the irony of ambition and attainment, vision and revision, and emancipation and illusion. This is done mostly by weaving out situations in a way that the responses of the characters to those situations reveal their contradictions. Flirtatious Etta was in her middle forties. Though "still the same — her hair blonde, her manner as lively, yet her admirers are fewer, fatter, and less ardent." But her Indian admirers subscribed to those fine values of which she alone, being a foreigner is the embodiment, so is Lalaji in the *Nature of Passion* (1956) who combines in him a deep sense of "religious duty" with the unscrupulousness of a businessman. He considers it wrong therefore to discard "bribery" as "corruption" because it is an indispensable courtesy and a respectable, civilized way of carrying on business.

In her second novel, *the Nature of Passion*, the situation becomes ironical even when tradition and environment become more and more incompatible. Nimmi, a modern girl who believes in emancipation, goes to clubs, plays tennis in shorts, keep bobbed hair dotes with boys and attends lectures almost ignorantly on English literature in fashionable clothes, but the family in which she lives is old and conservative. Phupiji, the real custodian of orthodoxy, used to say : "A girl of that age has no right to enjoy herself. She should be maintaining a household and bearing children and looking after her husband."[4 (Text)] Here the juxtaposition of the traditional mode of life against the modern accentuates not only the changes that have become perceptible in the cultural complex of the country but also the superficiality of the so-called modern life. Therefore, another character Viddi, does approve the cheap imitation of the Western mode of life. Viddi does not understand the essential difference, in terms of approach, atmosphere and attitude, between the Western and the Eastern modes of life. Viddi fails to draw a line of demarcation between the Western and the Eastern modes of life in terms of approach, atmosphere and attitude. He has an ambition to become either a writer or a critic, but when his father decides to pay five hundred rupees per month for looking after a shop he feels happy as it will reduce his financial burden. The casualness of his tone has made him the real man, irony of his character being the most poignantly brought out through this situation. He possesses similarity with his elder brother Om who has taken after his materialist father in spite of his taste for the glamour of high society. Kanta, his England-returned civil servant brother's wife and herself an intellectual snob, climaxes the ironic stance when she mistakes Viddi for Om at the picnic. As a matter of fact each one of the children of Lalaji, notwithstanding their emancipated thinking is a leech on him and is essentially a chip of the same block as his father. Mrs. Jhabvala brings out the implied irony by either comparing or juxtaposing situations. Through proper assessment the novelist evinces that the sons, daughters and the daughter-in-laws who claim to be modern against traditionalist Lalaji, are in essence self seeking parasites. Contrary to these moderns, Lalaji the conservative and materialist, although unrefined and unpretentious is more humane and sensible than them. The westernised son and the daughter-in-law make plan to save money from their own income and always ask the old man to pay for their children's fees, trips to the excursions. They practise duplicity on the straightforward patriarch. The same situation is seen in *The Householder* where a national of the West, known for pragmatism, advises the Indian lecturer to practise detachment. The irony becomes more effective when he, blissfully unaware of crushing miserable predicament, glibly reproduces in pompous tone what the *Gita* has said about the significance of contentment and resigned attitude in life. He sounds even ridiculous as he proffers this incongruous advice to lead purposeful life without explaining how without a sound economic base can plan to make his existence meaningful.

In *Esmond in India* (1958) there is a student of Indian culture and literature who scrapes his living by providing private lessons in Hindi and in Indian history and literature to English memsahibs, tourists, and elite Indian. He moves about in the "Culture Circuit" to deliver lectures and attend cock tail parties. His attractive speech has made Gulab to fall in love with him and gets married with him against the wishes of her parents. Gulab's habits, tastes and temperament are artistically depicted by the novelist in the beginning of the novel. The novelist presents so authentic and exact a picture of her Indian mode of life, and so sympathetically, that none will ever imagine that all this will be resented by her British husband. So when the novelist starts describing Esmond's indifference, antipathy and annoyance with his Indian wife, readers feel jolted. Afterwards, the novelist lingers on the irony of their relationship to substantiate her view : Gulab is lazy, she likes spicy food and sweets and hates furniture because they reduce space and hinder movement but Esmond detests all these habits. In him life matters just the opposite of what Gulab thinks and does. Although in love with Indian culture, he is unable to put up with such oddities. He actually hates her, despite her physical attraction and devotion, for spending much of her time with her mother and showing indifference to the food habits of her child. The dependence of the Indian woman on her mother for guidance in all matters pertaining to conjugal life makes him uncomfortable as he feels neglected by his consort. Consequently he drifts towards Betty who, "was light, modern and airy and being with her was almost as good as being England." His affection for India is thus mercenary. Similarly, Shakuntala's love for "Esmond the Don Juan" is sentimental. A romantic straight out of college and very much bohemian, fed on Byron and Shelley, she is in love with the idea of freedom. She permits herself to be seduced by the flamboyant Esmond in his hotel room. She is so infatuated with him that she raises him to heroic proportions even where he is irritated and embarrassed. She calls the loss of his shoes at the Taj Mahal a "momental tragedy as, she thought, it endowed peevish Esmond with great dignity in his angry solitude." Actually "he lacked an internal centre," as V.A. Shahane expresses, "because, among other things, the circumference of sensibility overwhelms him."[5] So the reaction of Betty to the same situation is different : first she giggles and then she laughs at his stupidity. Betty's reaction not only sets Shakuntala's exaggerated feelings in perspective but also exposes the hollowness of her education. In her infatuated blindness when Shakuntala entreats him to allow her to his "slane." She creates the anti-climax comparable with that created by incompatible Gulab who thought Esmond was her husband and therefore her "God." This Esmond, the idol of the two educated Indian females Shakuntala and Gulab, looks ridiculous ordering his servant in Hindustani — the language he was teaching — without realizing the irony that the listener "could not even identify the language he was speaking." Similarly, when he shouts at Gulab to condemn her for her wonderful propensity to squalor, he asks, ".... if pressed on the point would you call yourself a slut?" But surprisingly enough she does not understand the connotations of his abusive language. She does not respond to what he says. But when the servant endeavours to violate her chastity she feels strong embarrassment and leaves her husband without a moment's delay for not keeping her in ample protection.

The Householder deals with how the protagonist becomes absolutely helpless amidst the challenges of his circumstances.

Suffering from lower middle class complexities, the hero Prem experiences trouble in living on equal terms with his colleagues because his wife is a shy, simple and unsophisticated woman, and he faces constant economic problems. He does not easily tolerate that on the labour and income of householders students, her nuts and ascetics flourish whereas they suffer. The Ancient Sage Manu has expressed that the householder is pivotal of the society, so Prem willingly attempts to assess the modern way of life. Although as a professor in a college he is always aware of his dignity, he is faced with two immediate problems : first a hike in the salary and second reduction in the rent. He gets frustration in these attempts. So he likes to seek solace in spiritual pursuits. But even this alternative does not help him. Finally, through the surrender of his household to his domineering mother and temporary separation from his wife, he discovers that his malady is not as much economic as emotional when he sees that his wife is extremely passionate to him he feels that the hot dry season has come to an end and the monsoon rains has arrived. This irony is reinforced by the hollowness of the philosophical stances Prem takes while dealing with his people. While explaining the four stages of man's life, he expatiates on three stages with gusto, but seeing the *samosas* and the hot tea placed before him he quietly skippes the fourth stage, that is the stage of renunciation on the ground that he is not sure of that.

It is another irony that some foreigners — Hans and Kitty are good examples — refuse to listen to anything on India's economic and political achievements, and want to discuss the philosophy of Maya and Yoga. They do not believe that India is poor or deficient in any way so long as here the sun sets — the tigers — the women — and the songs are as good as anywhere else. Hans is of the view that Indians have only one problem they mortify flesh and grow soul. This appears name as it does from the mouth of a European speaker of truth who himself is a ludicrous figure with necksack rimless spectacles, loud voice and shorts.

Once again irony is evolved in *Get Ready for Battle* through the inadequacy of characters to live up to their own expectations. Sarla Devi, wife of a business shark, is an idealist and a reformer. She lives away from her husband, and her son lives away from her with his wife. When she learns that the poor people of Bundi Basti are likely to be ejected under the pretentious plan of slum clearance, she incites her son to fight the injustice : "Oh Vishnu, Vishnu why are you like that? You are like my son, you are as beautiful as Krishna and as strong as Arjun. But your conduct is that of a little merchant's son." She conducts her inspiring talk with her son in these words, "You must stand up son, fight, you must fling yourself into the world." Now she herself may be a skygazer with a heart overflowing with sympathy for the poor, but her son Vishnu in reality is only, "a little merchant's son." But she unaware of the implications, compares him with Krishna and Arjun on the ground that "he is her son." This inadequacy of assessment and description of her own son's qualities is all the more odd because she compares the cause of Bundi Basti people with that of the Pandavas of the Mahabharat. Judy, an English lady, marries an Indian youth in *A Backward Place*. Bal is a handsome young man of romantic temperament. He has attracted by the glamour of film heroes. For this he has spent the precious years of youth. He has neglected his responsibilities to his wife and two children. On the other hand, Judy is a wise soft-natured and understanding woman. She is mentally ready to compromise with life and helps her husband to regain confidence and uses his talent. But her patience with the jobless husband for ten years itself, despite being exemplary is fed on illusions like Bal's. The characters Gulab and Judy are contrasted. They belong not to different cultural backgrounds but they are also temperamentally different. May Judy, being modest, co-operative and accommodating, is cast in her own image by Mrs. Jhabvala who is herself married to an Indian architect. But the irony of her mistaken choice is prominently revealed. Etta, the symbol of practical wisdom, who hates everything Indian, advises her to leave her husband. But Judy does pay heed to it. She lives dreaming of a golden future. Their romanticism does not match with the circumstantial pressure. They are as unhappy as Gulab and Esmond in *Esmond in India* on account of incompatibility. Delhi, the locale of her novel, or for that matter the whole country, is "a backward place." Its poverty is appealing, but for the amelioration of the starving millions. Sudhir offers a solution, that is, he wants to run a professional theatre to educate people through entertainment. Jayaker, the old revolutionary who thinks there is no great cause to fight for after Independence asks Judy : Are you thinking of the masses? To bring joy and jollity — or perhaps culture and civilization into their drab lives? Thus, the novelist underlines the irony inherent in the suggestion. Sudhir's visualization of a better India with the elite, well bred high society, with cameramen moving about to take the photographs of speechmakers in glittering clothes sounds, incongruous with his own rudderless life, not unlike Bal's and many others. This blindness to reality, projected through Bal and Sudhir who are romantic and thorough "transitory visitors" of Europe, who come fascinated by the spiritual grandeur of India but plan to run back to their native habitat when they encounter economic backwardness, is the target for exposure by Mrs. Jhabvala in this novel. The most ironic thing is the tenacity with which Judy, in spite of all that she hears and knows about India decides to stay on with Bal. She understands better the country of her choice than others who come here for short period on tour, or those inside the country who come superficially under the impact of the West and try to condemn their own heritage to sound objective and modern. Finally, the young intellectual Sudhir, who has strayed after resigning a teaching job in Calcutta into the wrong kind of high-brow, heralds of cultural revolution, decides to go to the villages to work for the regeneration of the masses. Similarly, Judy decides to go to Bombay with Bal to help him try his luck in the film industry. Thus they accept this "backward place" whereas the other European expatriates like Etta and the Hahstadts could not come to terms with the reality of the place and leave for their homes at the earliest. Etta comes to India with a young Indian husband but soon after divorces him as she has deserted several husband earlier. Shy and promiscuous she prefers to go back to the unreal homeland of her nostalgic memories, whereas stability seeking modest Judy finds a lot in this "backward" place to live by and hope for.

In *A New Dominion*, the three girls, Lee, Margaret and Eve are mistaken for taking sex a medium of spiritual attainment. These girls come to India to seek spiritual solace from the frustrating materialistic life of their homeland, each wishing to be a new person, ultimately to quote V.A. Shahane, "Come to a sense of mutual jealousy among them as to their closeness of Swami."[6] The irony is that the truth seekers of the West end up by mistaking sex for spirituality, has been made the topic of discussion here.

The young narrator of Olivia's story in *Heat and Dust* expresses, "India always changes people, and I have been no exception." Olivia, an English lady, marries to an Anglo-Indian, comes to India in the thirties and falls for a prince. She dies of crude operation done on her by a quack to disturb her pregnancy. The young narrator herself — she has come to India to reconstruct the life of Olivia from details to be collected from persons and places associated with her — becomes a junior Olivia, she allows child, an Englishman turns Hindu who has "constant erections" to do her in so that she can reach a higher plane of consciousness through the power of sex. Margaret of *A New Dominion* dies as Divia is to die later in *Heat and Dust,* in very pathetic circumstances. She is not allowed by the Swamiji to be taken to hospital in the same way as Olivia is not taken to hospital by her lover prince till she dies. Whether India is "a new dominion", or a country of "heat and dust" it is "a backward place" for want of medical knowledge, economic stresses and bogus godmen. The novelist, despite her renewed attempts every time she writes a new novel to be objective continues to be sneering in her attitude. Martial dissonance in various shades, familial clashes between the old and the new generations, or the fallen state of spiritual mentors of modern India, all these situations finally help her project her own secret non-acceptance of the country for her adoption. In a rather blunt matter she expresses this in her autobiography : "However, I must admit that I am no longer interested in India. What I am interested now is myself in India"[7] (An Experience in India).

Besides these situations, there are many occasions in Mrs. Jhabvala's novel where verbal irony is employed to reveal the inner dynamics of her character's mind. No doubt, India is technologically and socially not so advanced, she attracts visitors from Western countries for her grand ancient culture. However, there are three major categories of those who come to India : One, those who study Indian literature and culture at their own universities and come on pilgrimage to the country of their interest

— Dr. Hochstadt is an example; second, those who fall in love with Indian culture and life and want to settle down here — Esmond and Judy are the best examples; third, those truth seekers who come to learn Yoga from Swamiji and spend their time in raising their Kundalini — the best example are Hans and Kutty. But those who come to India with genuine interest in her culture and her current regeneration are really few and far between. Therefore, the fourth category of those foreigners who, although placed here and in love with India hate her backwardness and poverty and always think of returning to their native countries — Etta and Betty are representative examples of this category. Thus in so far as the understanding and analysis of Western characters is concerned, Jhabvala's fiction is quite inclusive and extensive. But when it comes to portraying Indian characters, she tends to repeat certain types — knowledgeable but emotionally immature women like Shakuntala (*A Backward Place*) and Amrita *(To Whom She Will)*; fashionable wives of dignitaries without any understanding of their culture or current historical situation like Lady Ram Prasad *(To Whom She Will)* and Mrs. Kaul *(A Backward Place)*: and the custodians of the dead Indian tradition like Phupiji *(The Natrure of Passion)*, or the upholders of British education like Amrita's grandfather *(To Whom She Will)*, uncertain and confused youngmen like Hari and Krishna *(To Whom She Will)*. and Bal and Sudhir *(The Backward Place)*. Her Local is Delhi, the city of the old and the new, which is a microcosm of the sub-continent called India. But she does not cross the confines of the middle class life. Her grasp of the characteristic features of this life is certain, but the elaborations and repetitive details irritate the readers. Her ironic vision within her range is definitely revealing. There is no doubt about it. Her own life characterizes this irony when she speaks in her autobiography "An Experience in India", "I do sometimes go back to Europe. But after a time I get bored there and want to come back here. I also find it hard now to stand the European climate. I have got used to intense heat and seem to need it."[8]

NOTES AND REFERENCES

1. Narsimha, Raji, *Sensibility Under Stress : Aspects of Indo-English Fiction*, Ashajanak Prakashan, New Delhi, 1976, p. 138.

2. Meena, Belliappa, "A Study of Jhabvala's Fiction," *Banasthali Patrika*, Special Number on Indo-English Fiction, January 1969, p. 70.
3. Jhabvala, Ruth Prawer, *To Whom She Will,* Penguin Books, Ananda offset Private Ltd., Calcutta,1982, p. 78.
4. Jhabvala, Ruth Prawer, *The Nature of Passion*, Penguin Books, Ananda Offset Private Ltd., Calcutta, 1989, p. 83.
5. Shahane, V.A., *Ruth Prawar Jhabvala*, Arnold Heinemann Publication, New Delhi, 1976, p. 96.
6. Shahane, V.A., *Ruth Prawer Jhabvala*, Arnold Heinemann Publication, New Delhi, 1976, p. 118.
7. Jhabvala, Ruth Prawer, *Autobiography: An Experience in India,* Somaya Publication, Bombay, 1972, p. 41.
8. Jhabvala, Ruth Prawer, *Autobiography : An Experience In India,* Somaya Publication, Bombay, 1972, p. 48.

9

Nayantara Sahgal's *A Situation in New Delhi* : A Critical Study

—Chhote Lal Khatri

POLITICS is the favourite forte of Nayantara Sahgal in her novels. This provides a continuity to her novels. Her first novel *A Time to be Happy* (1958) and the next novel *This Time of Morning* (1965) are set in the post-Gandhian era and witness the collapse of Gandhism. *This Time of Morning* recaptulates the political evens in India in the last phase of Nehru's Prime Ministership. It is regarded as one of the best political novels in Indian English fiction. Her third novel *Storm in Chandigarh* (1969) is written in the backdrop of the partition of the Punjab into the Sikh-dominated Punjab and the Hindu dominated Haryana — both having the common capital Chandigarh. It shows how it results into unrest and violence in Chandigarh and how Harpal Singh and Gyan Singh, the Chief Ministers of Haryana and Punjab, respectively fall out over this contentious issue of the capital. *A Situation in New Delhi* (1977) takes into account the political scenerio after the end of Nehru's era. The image of Nehru is projected in the charismatic Prime Minister Shivaraj. Besides politics her novels have several things in common. Man-woman relationship, autobiographical bearings, the quest for identity, and urge for change are some of the common properties of her novels. In *A Situation in New Delhi* we find "the remarkable expose of politics and society in India complete with sham, hypocrisy, meanness, corruption and manipulations, the intrigues and the humbug." Nayantara also describes in vivid detail "the sexual adventures of Devi, Education Minister in the new cabinet after the death of her brother, Shivraj and the violent misadventures of her son, Rishad who firmly believes that India's problems can be solved only through violence..."[1]

The narrative centres round two characters : Devi, the Education Minister and her son, Rishad, a naxalite — both representing two different ways of life, two different methods of dealing with socio-political problems. Devi, the legacy of Shivaraj represents non-violent approach and Rishad who represents the frustration of the youth runs amok. Both want change and it is the question of change that occupies the centre stage in the discourses of the characters in this novel. Usman Ali, the Vice-Chancellor of Delhi University explains Devi who calls on him at his office when he is injured by errant mob of students :

'Where do your colleagues live, Shahbano? From the bullock cart to supersonic jet aircraft, hundreds of dams and canals, electrification for miles of village countryside, is quite a change. Even your colleagues must realize we've travelled some distance. The problems on our hands are the problems of change. And nowhere has it been so unwieldy as in education'[2] (p. 23).

What changes are required and where? How change should be brought out? These are some of the basic questions with which the novelist elaborately deals. The youth are rudderless and hence they go berserk in their pursuit for change. The Vice-Chancellor admits that the failure of leadership coupled with faulty educaitonal policy causes aberration in students' life. He goes deep into the problems and shows clear understanding of the situation and advocates delinking of degrees from jobs : "Universities can't be scattered like birdseed. It isn't possible to deal in ideas untill we become much more selective, and we can't do that if every job requires a degree" (pp. 22-23). But unfortunately he becomes the victim of violent mob of students over the expulsion of three students on the charge of rape of Madhu who later commits suicide because her 'middle class morality' does not allow her to continue with this defiled life. Devi, the Education Minister, who loves Usman shows her deep concern for the safety of Usman. But his anxiety is that those involved into anti-social activities are "Our own. Our children" (22). As we see that Rishad, Devi's son, one of the brilliant students, comes to believe that violence is the only means to bring about change and finally becomes the victim of the same violence himself. For the directionless youth it is no longer a question of the Gandhian philosophy of means over ends as Sahagal has depicted in *This Time of Morning* but that of ends justifying means. The urge to create an Indian Utopia, like George Orwells's Oceania, is too great to be suppressed. It acquires the proportion of cosmic tragedy arising out of misguidance and ignorance of human values. We feel sorry for Rishad who passionately believes in the cult of violence. As he says :

"Panic was like a gas. You could release it according to plan, in jets and spurts or in long slow expulsion, depending on what you intended... Rishad had not killed, though the first injunction was : if anyone saw you or tried to stop you, kill. Once they planned a killing, however, they used a suqad of twelve or thirteen-year-olds to do it, and trained them to do it scientifically. If possible, they supervised the finale themselves : ambush in a one-way street, the knife too swift to permit a cry, almost no blood...This cult of violence had to be clean, cold and disciplined, unaided by motive, by drugs or mental aberration. This was the violence of the sane with a passion for justice. To build a new world, the old one had to be razed to the ground. The way to do it was through the systematic creation of panic. Panic to chaos to ruin. And out of ruin open revolt and power. Only then could the new social order arise. Not Utopia. Just food in the stomach and a decent wage. Utopia for the poor and the downtrodden. An Indian Utopia" (p. 58).

The novel is not only an indictment against the Government's failure to formulate a new education policy but also against teachers and parents for not understanding their students and children and this gives way to communication gap. Nayantara Sahgal rightly believes that the government, social institutions and individuals have remained confined to their own walls and have created an air of alienation which the young cannot bear. Rishad is so walled up with his own ideas that he keeps himself aloof from his mother's engagements, from family functions like marriage, party etc. Devi who finds little time for him, attributes his extraordinary outer reserve to the time when he was born :

"Caught between ancient myth and industrial present, it was

no wonder if any young or even older person found life a little bewildering" (p. 18).

Sahgal has portrayed Rishad as a typical product of his elitist background and Western education. When Devi asks Rishad to attend Pinky's engagement party he says refusing it :

'What in the world will I do there? Besides, that kind of marriage is just organized rape.' One way or another the hideous word kept figuring in her day. 'Pinky hasn't been allowed to put her nose out of the house without her mother's permission. And now they're handing her over like a pudding to that nitwit who hasn't put his nose out of his house — his mental nose anyway. Talk about rape at the university. I think this is quite obscene' (p. 25).

Incidently it echoes Rajneesh's reaction on arranged marriage; he calls it 'licensed prostitution'. Sahgal in may respects wants to break the edifice of traditional Indian life. In *This Time of Morning* Sahgal finds fault with the Indian parenthood which demands obedience and respect for their elders"[3] (p. 51) and neglects 'the most important potential in our country, our young' (p. 52)[4]. *In A Situation in New Delhi* Devi never imposes her views, desires on her son. They have their 'own line of battle and neither crosses' (25). But what is the result? A spoilt child. Both represent two aspects of the same problem of change. The Education Ministry wants change in curriculum of studies and in the whole education policy to channelise this abundant energy into the right direction. Rishad is facing the problem in his own way. He wants to bring overnight radical change in the rotten system :

"The main thing to remember is that there's no room for philosophy where there's hunger and terrible inequality. There's only room for surgery to remove them, and they have to be removed, like a cancer, like filth — he made an incisive gesture followed by her startled eyes, 'in any way at all', with any weapon. The only way that will not work is with words. There have been enough words, We have to act" (p. 66).

After Shivraj's death Devi is inducted in the ministry just to show allegiance to Shivraj. But Devi finds that Shivraj's friends and followers 'who had written paeans of praise to him' have turned against him and his ideals. She feels herself alien in the Government. Lakshmi Sinha rightly observes that "Devi's hold on her ministry is as inconsequential as her influence over her son Rishad."[5] That is why she failes to get Usman's new education policy passed by the Government. She feels so cornered that she seeks solace in the company of Usman. Devi is so absorbed in her obligation to her brother Shivraj, his life and fame that she "seemed all given to her brother, his life, his needs. She had no other life" (52).

Her short, lived married life with Ishwar doesnot quench her emotional and physical thirst. She develops relations first with Michael and then with Usman. But she is so obsessed with her loyality to Shivraj that she cannot continue her sexual relations with Michael. The physical intimacy with them provides her a kind of 'emotional release.'[6] However, one may say that she lacks the courage and moral strength to fight for the values upheld by Shivraj and ultimately resigns from the cabinet.

The changes in the post Shivraj era are depicted through two other characters also namely Michael Clavert, journalist and biographer and Usman Ali besides Devi and Rishad. Both Michael and Usman had been close to Shivraj and remained under the spell of his charismatic personality and leadership even after his death. Sahgal's preference for Nehru is clearly reflected in the presentation of Shivaraj. She makes him reviewed by a foreigner-Michael and a Muslim-Usman. The novel begins with Michael's shock and weeping on reading the news of Shivraj's death. He regards him as an Asian not an Indian and says that "there is not going to be another like him in a hundred years" (6). Again when the Vice-Chancellor's office is sabotaged and he is injured, he greatly misses Shivraj for his leadership quality :

"Shivraj had the gift of putting things in perspective, and since his death Usman had become convinced that was leadership's main task. To put into perspective. To gather up the facts and fevers and strands, the achievements and the discouragement and place it where it could be seen against the whole, the past, the future" (p. 28).

After Shivraj's death the country faces a serious problem of leadership — a vacuum has been created. The next Prime Minister has nothing of Shivraj's quality and the real power is exercised by the Minister for Mines. Devi, too, has no such leadership quality. That is why Rishad is drawn towards Naren, a naxalite leader and not towards Devi. His hero-worship is so acute that he watches Naren lying sick with injuries given to him by the police with admiration and sadness. The same crisis of leadership is evident in her other novels also. Like Shivraj, the death of the old Home Minister in *Storm in Chandigarh* causes a vacuum. In *The Day in Shadows* — Sahgal depicts the rise of unscruplous, sex maniac as leader after the death of the Minister for Petroleum.

In the quest for change and for leadership. Sahgal brings to fore two unique characters in this novel : Skinny Jaipal and Usman in his new role. Usman resigns from office, takes up the challenge of providing leadership to the students. In his confession of failure, in his relation with his wife, Nadira, he emerges as the most honest of Sahgal's characters :

"There was a peculiar humiliation in not being able to convey your truth, your essential personality to the person who lived under your roof, shared your bed, saw you in all your unguarded nakedness every single day : the person who had more evidence to condemn you than any other had, but who also had glimpses into your striving, your efforts at bravery. Who else saw any of that, and why should the debit side alone figure in the summing up? Yet really the failure was his. Wherever he might have succeeded, with Nadira he had failed. May be she had erected an Islamic fortress around her, imprisoned herself, a princess in a tower. But he had failed to reach her and the failure was his" (p. 137).

Skinny Jawipal is a unique creation of Sahgal for she combines in herself the characteristics of two opposites — tradition and modernity. She however appears more modern than conventional in her approach to life. She has the shyness and devotion to Indian culture, to her study, music and dance of a traditional girl. But as a modern girl she has no qualms about joining Rishad's group in his revolution to shock people into action. She has no problem in being kissed at Pinky's party or in having sex with Rishad. She is eager to learn and contribute her part to the well-needed social change. She goes to the cemetery on his call for initiation into his group. But she is way ahead in the genuineness of the revolutionary concepts. She stands in contrast with Rishad in the basic philosophy of revolution. She believes that revolution begins with the self whereas for Rishad revolution is for others. She carries out the first gruesome raid in her own house and destroys her dead mother's clothes and possessions. And yet she is normal. Rishad can't do the same. Lakshmi Sinha rightly believes that Sahgal has taken up the two images — *Abla* and *Shakti*[7] of conventional Indian women and forms the image of *Sabla* in the character of Skinny Jaipal. Nayantara Sahgal, too remarks in the same vein in letter to Jasbir Jain :

"I try to create the virtuous women — the modern Sita, if you like, my women are strivers and aspirers, towards freedom, towards goodness, toward a compassionate world. There virtue is a quality of heart and mind and spirit, a kind of untouched innocence and integrity, I think there is this quality in the Indian women"[8] (145).

Unlike Devi she has strong determination and courage of conviction. She quickly understands that Rishad is treading a wrong and disastrous path in the name of revolution and brings to him a new realisation with love and care. She releases him from his ideological burden and he sees the sky overhead peaceful :

"The future was not all sorted out but at least some of it was clearer. He and Priya had talked, and without ever using the word love they had pledged themselves to something bigger even than their love for each other... Priya had demonstrated the first time he met her that revolution begins with oneself, is not a lesson given to others. Some blindness had prevented him from seeing the obvious and making the only contribution that could matter : a clean break with the life he led, an end to this sterile intellectual participation, and a going over to the other side. He did not know yet where that meant going but he knew he would never, as long as he lived, go back to the life he lived" (p. 146).

Unfortunately Rishad's death comes so suddenly that he does not find time to come to terms with the world under her loving supervision. However, with the new realisation Rishad is determined to become leader himself and to convince Naren and his followers of what he had discovered. In his new role he makes a desperate attempt to dissuade his group from isolated acts of violence but he fails and is killed. The truth of non-violence ultimately dawns on him. This shows Sahgal's belief in non-violent means to achieve the desired change in the system.

It won't be amiss to add here a brief comment on the narrative technique of this novel. The subject is so impersonal and topical that Sahgal employs a third person omniscient narrator in *A Situation in New Delhi* as if she is a detached observer of the hell going on in the corridors of power in Delhi. Being the niece of Pandit Jawahar Lal Nehru, she watches the whole things from a close quarter. She chooses the world with which she is most conversant and hence her narrative has a stamp of authenticity. The third persons narrative method allows her to give into the minds of her characters and present her views on men and matters. She relates vividly social and political life of elite class — concerts, party, dance and music, political gossips and amorous relationships of Devi in elitist language. But there is a marked understatement in the portrayal of bed scenes. The method helps her gain objectivity and panoramic view of the situation in New Delhi : but at the cost of emotional entensity and involvement on the part of the readers. Its readability is slightly affected because of abrupt digressions. The novel consists of sixteen sections and most of which are unsequential but related to the plot. In the first section we are told about the death of Shivraj, Michael's shock over it and his preparation to return to India on a mission of writing a book on Shivraj. We are given no view of his death scene, not even Devi's reaction. The second section begins with Devi's preparation for party :

"When Devi opened her eyes her first drowsy thought was that she has noting suitable to wear to the party she was attending that night..." (p.14).

It does not sound very convincing. Again Devi's relationships with Michael, Usman, and her calendestine love affairs with them are unhealthy and unrealistic. Her relationship with Shivraj is too idealistic and unbecoming of either a feminine model or an Indian woman. However, she describes Devi's predicament in realistic terms. She neither fights for Shivraj's cause nor shakes herself off the ghost of Shivraj. Usman tells her :

"My poor Shahbano, you are very out of date, demanding clarity. The world has moved on into a frightful full of ideas and emotions all clogged up. Catch up with it or come with me" (132).

The husband-wife relationship (Usman and Nadira) has been portrayed in a conventional mould. Nadira is conformist and remains a devout Muslim wife despite knowing her husband's attraction for Devi. Their superficial relationship in the beginning gets deeper towards the end of the novel when Usman realises her need in the hour of crisis, when he resigns from office, and takes up a new challenge of leading the students. Though she cannot look beyond the ambit of religion and insists on leaving India, she compromises with her husband.

Through Michael who is visiting India after Shivraj's death the narrator makes him reflect on the past also. He recalls of the days before independence, Shivraj's leadership in those days and during his Prime Ministership and feels a sea change in the present. He is critical of censorship of press and religious intolerance. When his book is subjected to government's scrutiny, he feels that Shivraj is dead in both body and spirit. But the only hope lies in Usman's movement who proclaims :

"I see something taking shape and it has the face of chaos. We've got to avert that. I think I can if I can take the students with me. I've already discussed it with some of them and with a number of faculty members. We can make Delhi the laboratory of this experiment. If your Cabinet turns it down I'm going to campaign for it in the streets with the students" (p. 115).

Thus, Usman, a true patriot, leads the youth in Shivraj's footsteps in his quest to provide leadership to the country, in his mission to revive the values Gandhi and Nehru stood for. At least he keeps the flame of home burning and is rightly symbolised by Michael as a Christ in this chaos who is sitting on the top of a mountain and talking to the people like Christ's Sermon on the Mount.

REFERENCES

1. Comment on the Jacket of the novel.
2. Nayantara Sahgal : *A Situation in New Delhi*, 1977, New Delhi, Himalaya Books.
3. Nayantara Sahgal : *This Time of Morning*, 1965, London, Victor Gollanca.
4. *Ibid.*
5. Lakshmi Sinha : *Nayantara Sahgal's Novels : A Critical Study*, 1999, Patna Janaki Prakashan.
6. K. Meera Bai : *Women's Voices*, 1996, New Delhi Prestige Books.
7. Lakshmi Singh : *Nayantara Sahgal's Novels : A Critical Study*, 1999, Patna : Janaki Prakashan.
8. Quoted by Jasbir Jain in *Nayantara Sahgal*, 1978, New Delhi. Arnold Heinemann.

10

Sound of the Silenced : Shashi Deshpande's *That Long Silence*

—*Dr. Arati Biswal*

"Words are often no more than
silence, and silence has its voices."

SILENCE, in Shashi Deshpande's novel, is a key metaphor to an understanding of the text. It is a significant work in the sense that with this novel Deshpande breaks her own silence. She finds an affinity with Jaya, its protagonist. In a first person account, she confesses, "A lifetime of introspection went into this novel, the most autobiographical of all my writing, not in the personal details but in the thinking and ideas .... It was with the articulation of all that had been in me through the years that I came to feminism, to a consciousness of myself as a feminist" (107).

Jaya's silence is a part of, as Elizabeth Robin's asserts, "the weight of that long silence of one-half of the world" (Quoted in *That Long Silence)*. Though self-imposed, it is similar to the fate suffered by a majority of women all the world over. Silence is a suppressive device. It signifies death. It also means long, untold suffering, mostly mental, which ultimately overcomes the need to express one's thought as an individual. It negates the self. The metaphor suggests withdrawal. That Long Silence reverbates with many silences, some imposed on the characters by long standing social mores and others embarked upon willingly.

The midlife crisis that Jaya, the urbanised middle-class housewife undergoes, is set on by the personal disaster that befalls the family. Mohan, her husband, commits an act of dishonesty and seeks temporary absence from his job till exonerated. The couple move into the seclusion of their Dadar flat and the children are sent away on vacation with friends. Jaya finds herself in a void. Freed momentarily from the drudgery that had become her life, she confronts the ghost of her "old self." Jaya realises "the nothingness of what had seemed a busy and full life" (25). In her enthusiasm to play the role of wife and mother to perfection, she finds she has obliterated that self in her, which as a child, was "heady with the excitement of finding unexpected resources within herself" (187). Jaya confesses to Mukta, her neighbour, "Without Mohan ... I don't know what I am" (185). For Jaya, this is the beginning of a crises in identity.

As Jaya picks up the threads of her past and tries to connect it with her present, she recollects the triumph with her present, with which her father had named her Jaya, "Jaya for Victory." Her father's death ironically, symbolised the beginning of her defeat. It brings a *volte face* in her life. Marriage and the customary renaming of Indian woman in their in-law's family snaps the name-linked identity with a finality. Jaya is renamed Suhasini. Jaya reminisces, "And I was Jaya. But I had been Suhasini as well... the Suhasini who was distinct from Jaya, a soft, smiling, placid, motherly woman. A woman who lovingly nurtured her family. A woman who cope" (16). This conflict between her dual identities leaves her confused and uncertain.

Jaya's conviction that communication between Mohan and herself, as man and woman, as two individual entities, was impossible, leads her to retreat into silence because, "It was so much simpler to say nothing, so much less complicated" (99). Security, the middle-class ideal, has silenced her. By accepting social and familial roles imposed upon her she has eclipsed her own needs. Jaya's situation reminds her of the "stillness, the silence" of sitting in a stationery train. The illusion of movement is created when the train next to hers moves. Deshpande uses the image effectively to indicate that activity and meaning in a woman's life are directly related to the needs of the man in her life. Jaya surmises, "Your own movement has been illusion. You were right where you were all along" (24).

Her mother's warnings in childhood have conditioned Jaya into thinking that silent submission is the only way to fulfilment. The questions and retorts have been smothered by the silence in which she takes refuge. But, "silences distort the truth," observes De Beauvoir (5). Jaya is schooled how to keep her anger and emotions in leash. She has been goaded to think that it is a sin for a woman to raise her voice against her husband. Mohan warns her, "My mother never raised her voice against my father, however badly he behaved to her" (83). Anger and other human emotions made a woman, unwomanly. Jaya silences the "frenetic emotions" in her as it had seemed "like a disease, a disability I had to hide from everyone" (97). Jaya remains silent on other counts too that affect her : her father's death, her wish to take up a job, her aborted child, her relationship with Kamat. Silence becomes the leit motif of her life. As a writer, Jaya has been guilty of silencing "other women." She plays safe by penning a fortnightly column "Seeta", light, humorous pieces about the travails of a middle-class housewife, " Nothing serious..." (149). She does not write about "women I had known ... because they might, it was just possible — resemble Mohan's mother, or aunt, or my mother or aunt (149). She is afraid of hurting family sentiments and this turning away from reality posits failure.

Jaya's brief interlude with Kamat, is her watershed. The relationship begins as a chance encounter at their Dadar flat on the first occasion, when after their marriage, Mohan and Jaya, come to live there. Kamat is a loner whose life is, as Jaya remarks, "structured to loneliness" (157), as he does not wish to concede any woman power over him. She finds in Kamat an echo of her inner voice. He is, as it were, her *alter-ego*. Jaya feels a compulsive urge to reveal her thoughts before him and a need for his companionship, "I had needed him" (146). He is another Zarathustra who urges her to be fearless, to vent her anger — to be herself.

Kamat warns Jaya of her "women are the victims" theory, her sense of self-pity and insists, "Take yourself seriously, woman. Don't skulk behind a false name. And work — work if you want others to take you seriously" (148). Jaya comes out of her self-deception. Her personal odyssey begins with the realisation that it is not Mohan who has restricted her or her marriage, but her own fears, fears of hurting family sentiments and fear of failure or "fear of flying." Kamat insists, "if you don't commit yourself, you'll never fail" (150).

As an iconoclast, Kamat urges Jaya to break free of her complexes. Under his tutelage, Jaya realises that she has to exorcise the fears that have made her, "the stereotype of a woman ... needing male help and support" (76). The unmasking begins with her serious writing. She is no longer a housewife writing to while away her time but a writer with commitment and firm conviction.

After Kamat's death and their return to the Dadar flat, Jaya finds the same doubts, rising again. It was before Kamat that she broke her silence. With other men it was different. With them, "It was already made clear that we were not on the same level," but with Kamat, "with this man I had not been a woman. I had been just myself — Jaya" (153). Kamat treats her as an equal, leading Jaya to shed her inhibitions. Jaya is brought out of her darkness into an open space by Kamat. She sees the underlying hollowness and deceit in her relationship with Mohan. It is a meaningless exercise of living together, "we lived together but there had been only emptiness between us" (185). Marriage has made her circumspect. As her mentor, Kamat had initiated her into serious writing. Jaya has found release through her writing. She has exorcised the fear that led to self-effacement, "Yes, I have been scared, scared of breaking through the veneer of a happy family" (191). With her panic groan she opens the door on all "those other women" — who really exist and whose silences underscored the pains of suffering womanhood.

Jaya picks up the strands of her life, past and present, and by connecting, comes to terms with the self in her. The chiaroscuro of events in her emerges "a multicoloured patchwork quilt" (188). She rejects the image of Mohan and herself as "a pair of bullocks yoked together." Her awareness of an unjust system that coerces a woman to ply second fiddle; to accept the position as an inferior being brings in her a sense of outrage that ruefully reminds her of rigid rules of Sanskrit drama that forced women to speak Prakrit, while reserving the classical Sanskrit for the superior male characters. Jaya refuses to concede to Mohan the authority he wielded over her earlier. She reiterates, "I'm Mohan's wife, I had thought, and cut off the bits of me that had refused to be Mohan's wife. Now I know that kind of a fragmentation is not possible" (191).

Jaya makes her choice by deciding to "erase the silence" between Mohan and herself "I will have to speak, to listen, I will have to erase the silence between us" (192), says Jaya. There is hope, even though change comes slowly. In making her choice she knows that "life has always to be made possible" (193), Jaya breaks through her illusion in an attempt to exist as an "absolute being."

Though Jaya breaks through her silence, other women characters in the novel are victims of their silence, allowing it to smother their latent desires. Her mother-in-law Vimala, her sister-in-law and Jeejabai, the domestic help, silently suffer the injustice of mail oppression. Jaya unmasks herself and relinquishes a silent martyrdom. In Jaya, the dual aspects of the feminine consciousness — one accepting male definition and identity, and the other, the androgynous aspect that revolts against male-imposed traditional constraints, is seen. Jaya's struggle to regain her freedom, to live life on her own terms is her attempt to establish her "rear' self.

Though Deshpande has her reservation about being called a "feminist" or "woman writer", she admits that her writings emerge from her "own intense and long suppressed feelings about what it is to be a woman in our society." She admits, "out of the experience of the difficulty of playing different roles enjoined on me by society, out of the knowledge that I am something more and something different from the sum total of these roles," her writing emerges. "My writing comes out my consciousness of the conflict between my idea of myself as a human being and the idea that society has of me as a woman" (2). Jaya, her protagonist in *That Long Silence* tries to resolve this conflict between her "idea of herself' and the idea that society upholds of her "as a woman," by emerging from the trapped situation — husband, children, work — which she has helped create, despite herself. She breaks out of the Nora syndrome.

Jaya's experience is universal. This is evident from the recent review of a study of women facing midlife crisis, Terri Apter's *Secret Paths : Women in the New Midlife.* This study indicates that many women are troubled by the fact that they did have choices. The route out of their crisis suggested is that they stop focusing on missed opportunities and take up those still on offer. By turning protester, by resisting, Jaya translates her feeling of inadequacy into a better idea of what she wants.

WORKS CITED

Beauvoir, Simone De. *Force of Circumstance,* Harmondsworth: Penguin, 1983.

Bradberry, Grace. "The Very Valuable Crisis," *The Statesman*, 13 May, 1979 : 9.

Deshpande, Sashi. "Of Concerns, Of Anxieties," *Indian Literature,* vol. XXXIX, no. 5 (Sept.-Oct., 1996), p. 107.

— *That Long Silence,* New Delhi : Penguin, 1989.

11

Her Life Is Her Own

—Darshana Trivedi

> You are your own refuge;
> there is no other refuge;
> This refuge is hard to achieve.
>
> *—The Dhammapada*

THE Dark Holds No Terrors (1980) is Shashi Deshpande's first novel and as she herself says, "*The Dark Holds No Terrors* is, of all my novels, the one dearest to me." *Hindustan Times* hailed Deshpande's art of story telling with these words, "an extremely talented story teller with an uncommon way with words." The novel presents a realistic plight of a middle class woman torn between two roles — traditional and modern, between inner duties and outer duties, between family and profession. Her female characters Indu, Jaya, and Sarita respectively from *Roots and Shadows, That Long Silence and The Dark Holds No Terrors* are ordinary middle class women, down to earth and face crisis of life silently and internally. The women of Anita Desai and Nayantara Sahgal belong to a slightly upper strata of society, whereas Deshpande portrays the average middle class woman with her deeply felt but never so well expressed experience of life's little ironies. Her image of woman is neither an old orthodox, nor a westernized woman but every woman of India economically independent, emotionally dependent.

Since ages woman is considered to be the shadow of man — no dreams of her own, no desires of her own, no life of her own. Her voice remains unsung throughout the ages. The only aim of her life is to obey and follow the command of her husband as it is said, "Pitru Vakya Janardanam," the Father's will or the husband's will is the will of God. As Manu said :

> Day and night women must be kept in subordination to the males of the family, in childhood to the father, in youth to her husband, in old age to her sons.....
>
> Eventhough the husband be destitute of virtue and seeks pleasure elsewhere he must be worshipped as god.[1]

Various religions and various societies have their own ideologies about woman. Digamber Jain religion believes : "Women can never attain salvation except by being reborn as men." Swaminarayan saints even today do not see the face of woman for their own religious reasons. The woman was excluded even from Vedic learning in ancient times. The condition of woman from centuries is like a sudra, a polluted and untouchable. In male-dominated society man is at the centre and woman is at the periphery. She has no choice, no identity and her pride lies only in suffering quietly without asking why?

As Shri Radhakrishna Says :

> Centuries of tradition have made the Indian woman the most patient woman in the world, whose pride is suffering.[2]

The blessings which she receives from the elders at the time of marriage since the past till the present, are "Akhand Saubhayavati bhav" *i.e.*, she must die before her husband and that is considered to be an auspicious for woman and if by God's will she fails to die before her husband, either she has to burn herself in the fire and acquires the title of "Sati" or to live the life of a widow even worse than a beast. Thus, an Indian woman in all the phases of life faces an ordeal of fire.

It is after the coming of Raja Rammohan Ray and Jotiba Phule, the social reformers, who made efforts to abolish the Sati tradition; Gandhiji, a man much ahead of his time, who considered woman as Ardhangini, Sahdharmcharini or a companion in the real sense and Western Liberal education which forced new values and norms of life that new space and new roles were created for woman. The woman now is economically independent, professional and modern. Deshpande presents the crisis of an ordinary middle class professional woman and poses three questions : are they really happy with modern situation? Can Economic independence make them individual in the true sense? Are they really *equal* to man?

The Dark Holds No Terrors begins with Sarita's home coming, knocking at the door of her Krishna's place. At this time she remembers the story of Krishna and Sudama. Though apparently there is no similarity between Sarita and Sudama as she says : "She herself was certainly no Sudama in rags, barefeet and humility she had none of these" (15) yet her story is related to Sudama who came to Lord Krishna with the problem of deprivation but said not a word about it. Saru, like Sudama, faces the crisis of life though differently. The home coming helps her to sort out her problems. In the quiet repose of her father's company she analyses, reviews and re-examines her life. Apparently she comes home to take care of her father because her mother is dead, but in reality, she wants to escape from the "nightmarish brutality" of her husband. Sarita's mother has no sympathy for her for she was unable to save her brother Dhruva — the only male child in the family from drowning in the pond. Sarita remembers the lifeless and harsh words even after her mother's death ; "Why didn't you die? why are you alive and he dead?" (34). This is the plight not only of Saru but millions who are born as girls. The fault lies with their gender not with them. The male child is considered to be superior for he will rite the funeral pyre and perform all rites including "Shraddha," Saru's mother, Kamala is an orthodox, traditional woman throughout her life fails to understand Saru's psyche. The relationship between Baba, Saru and mother is like, "the three points of a triangle, eternally linked forever separate" (141). Saru — an ugly daughter of a beautiful mother is nothing but a constant burden to her. She wants to make Saru also a submissive woman like her and for her Dhruva — a son only matters as she says :

Don't go out in the sun
You will get even darker
Who cares?
We have to care if you don't

> *We have to get you married.*
> *I don't want to get married.*
> *will you live with us all your life?*
> *why not?*
> *You can't*
> *And Dhruva?*
> *He's different. He is a boy (45).*

The gender difference in her mother's treatment of Saru and Dhruva enrages Saru. She rebels against her "*If You're a woman. I do not want to be one*" (63). She rejects the traditional role of a woman.

> Our homes, our children, their schools, our possessions, our ideas..... these were the drab uniforms we wore, all the same dull colour. I didn't want to be one of them. I wouldn't be one of them. (157)

And this is the dark spot which kept Sarita far from love and sympathy from her family. Alienated and neglected as a child Saru decided to do something in life to be a successful woman, to prove and assert herself in the world. She leaves all her pleasures, dedicated to the study, scores sixtyfive percentage and joins medical college in Bombay against her mother's will.

During her study she meets a college mate Manohar, a poet and drama director. Her marriage with Manu is an assertion and affirmation of her feminine sensibility. She marries against the will of her mother who concerns about the caste identity of the boy and she asks her;

> *What caste is he?*
> *I don't know*
> *A Brahmin?*
> *of course, not*
> *Then cruelty...his father*
> *keep a cycle shop.*
> *Oh, so they are low-caste people, artehey? (96).*

Her marriage with Manu breaks all the barriers of social systems, the caste identity and the system of arranged marriage in which it is not the girl but girl's father who decides to whom she is going to marry. But after marriage she becomes a doctor and the situation changes. He had been the young man and I his bride now, I was the lady doctor and he was my husband (42). Now, she is a successful woman, earns not only butter but bread for the family (35). It is this open assertion made through an interview given for a special issue of a periodical on career women. When the interviewer jokingly mentions bread and butter, the ball of destruction of their relationship is set rolling and acquires momentum. Manu, a representative of the patriarchal society cannot bear the success of his wife. "And so the esteem with which I was surrounded made me inches taller. But perhaps the same thing that made me inches shorter" (42). After that incident Manu becomes "green eyed monster" at that night.

> "He attacked me like an animal that night. I was sleeping and I woke up and there was this....this man hurting me. With his hands, his teeth, his whole body. And this happen again and again till she lost the count of it" (201).

Sarup realizes that Manu though an educated modern man proves to be a traditional husband, the monarch of the family. After the repeated physical assault Saru cannot speak. She suffers silently. As she says :

> I put another brick on the wall of silence between us. May be one day I will be walled alive within it and die a slow, painful death (96).

Saru's feminine psyche becomes an arena of several forces. She is torn between her obligation to her profession as a doctor and her duties to her family. Caught between two roles she desires to leave her job. "Manu, I want to stop working. I want to give it all up my practice, the hospital everything" (79). But Manu denied it since it will bring down their standard of living. "On my salary? come on Saru, don't be silly. You know how much I earn" (81). On the one hand Manu desires her financial support while on the other hand he wants her to be "an angel of the home." This is impossible for Saru — not only for Saru but for any professional woman.

Virgina Woolf in her book *A Room of One's Own* which is considered to be the Bible of feminism by critics talks about two conditions for a woman a room of one's own and in income of one's own. Saru refers to these two conditions and related with the phase to her own life and thought.

> My mother had no room of her own. She retreated into the kitchen to dress up, she sat in this dingy room to comb her hair and apply *kumkum*, she slept in her bed like any overnight guest in a strange place. And I have so much my mother lacked. But neither she nor I have that thing "a room of our own" (135-36).

Saru here focucses on the realistic plight of an Indian middle class woman who is still the "Secondary citizen" in society.

While discussing about Saru's emotional crisis Deshpande discusses three different women characters and their attitudes to life. Saru, Smita and Nalu known as "Three Musketeers" (117) among friends represent three different phases of feminism. Smita, after marriage, turns into Geetanjali, has lost her own identity. She is just a wife, mother and only a house keeper a traditional "Gruhlaxmi image." Nalu is a spinster and dedicated to her job of teaching at the college. She preserves "an individual identity of a modern woman." To her, every problem is a women's problem and is bitter to everything and every body an extremist view of feminism. Saru combines both the images of woman a traditional and modern. Her problem is not only a woman's problem, a feminist problem but a problem for both the husband and the wife — the problem of society.

The author very suggestively uses the device of rain to clear the clouds of doubts, fears and uncertainties to achieve the catharsis for Saru to remove her guilt consciousness and attain the light of innocence. It's going to rain (210) and after the rain there is complete renewal in nature and in Saru.

> There was a smell of wet earth and rotting leaves. The trees, their dusty dirty leaves, washed by the rains to a tender sparkling green, were like symbols of renewal. It's over, she thought. That's done with. He is all right. Things will be all right now (211).

Saru's feeling of guilt and crisis is over. She can see the things in reality as her father says "Don't turn your back on things again.

Turn round and look at them. Meet him" (216) and with new confidence and renewed spirit she tells her father, "And, Oh yes Baba, if Manu comes tell him to wait. I'll be back as soon as I can" (221).

Saru's journey from self-alienation to self-identification from negation to assertion and from diffidence to confidence conpletes here. She prepares herself to confront reality not to escape from it. She, like Sudama, steps out in the world calmly and courageously.

The novel begins with the knocking at the door and ends with the knocking at the door. The first knock finds the entry into the inner journey of Saru's life and the last knocks enacts with the assertion "the dark holds no Terrors." Saru is now a rejuvenated new and integrated woman, an embodiment of strength and grace. She realizes that

> My Life is my own... Somehow she felt as if she had found it now, the connecting link. It Means you are not just a strutting, grimacing puppet, standing futilely on the stage for a brief while between areas of darkness. If I have been a puppet it is because I made myself one. I have been clinging to the tenuous shadow of a marriage whose substance has long since disintegrated because I have been afraid of proving my mother right (220).

NOTES

1. *Hunter College Women's Studies Collective : Women's Realities, Women's Choices : An Introduction to Women's Studies* (New York : Oxford University Press, 1983), 83.
2. Promilla Kapur, *The Changing Status of the Working Woman in India* (Delhi : Vikas, 1974), 366.

EDITION CITED

Deshpande, Shashi, *The Dark Holds No Terrors* (Delhi : Penguin, 1990).

12

Anita Desai's *In Custody* : Deven's Agony and Ecstasy

—*Dr. Sharada Iyer*

IN her novels, Anita Desai has concentrated more on characters rather than social milieu. They are not types, but individual men and women — the solitary beings — who have retreated, or driven into some extremity of despair, and so turned against or made to stand against the general current of life. Her characters, independent, agonized, frustrated, somewhat domineering combat with angry defiance, their individual problems and predicaments, which are basically existentialist. To Anita Desai, the action, the plot and the development of the novel are determined by the character, and the subject *In Custody* is Deven Sharma.

The novel unfolds the story of credulous and disingenuous Deven Sharma, who is swayed by an idea of creating a work of his life time, but is unfortunately defeated by his own helplessness. A temporary lecturer in Hindi in a private collge in Mirpore, a suburb of Delhi, Deven is interested in Urdu literature. As the novel opens, his friend Murad, editor of the Urdu magazine, 'Awaz', requests Deven to interview Nur Shahjehanbadi, a great Urdu poet, for a special number of his forthcoming issue. "Deven's hand fluttered on his knee as he melted at the suggestion and felt a glow creep through him at the thought of writing something in the language which had been his first language. The glow was also caused by pride... at being asked to contribute a piece by the editor of what he took to be a leading Urdu journal" (*IC,* p. 16). The rest of the narrative shifts between Deven's success and failure, his enthusiasm and hesitance, and the final disaster he lands into. Various forces work to help and defeat him, till finally he stands at a cross road, not knowing where to turn to. In the end he finds strength in his innerself and resolves to face life as it comes to him.

The prime chracteristics of Deven that attracts our attention are his helplessness, humility, suffering and nobility. Socio-economic factors, colour his personality and mould his psyche. The son of a debilitated, asthmatic school teacher, Deven belongs to a lower middle class family. As a child, he had watched closely the bitter disappointment of his mother, and the apologetic smile of his father for his failure in measuring upto her expectations. Obviously these familial and social factors generated in him a complaint and submissive tendency. Deven is one born to be bullied. He finds neither respect nor consideration from his colleagues, students nor neighbours. His wife, Sarla, is stupid, disappointed in her romantically silly notion of what marriage would bring. His idealised image of himself is that of an upright teacher in the college, a humble man in society and a victimized self at home, turning aggressive.

The repressive atmosphere of a lower middle class ethos offers him no suitable avenues of recognition. He is a gifted young man whose imagination has been fired by the glories of Urdu poetry. Deven engaged in the struggle for daily survival has shelved his artistic involvements and concerns. Having made his choices early in life he knows he has a salary to earn and a wife to support, but the world of poetry beckons him. Perhaps Murad's is the only way to get him to do something.

Deven is aware of his personal incompetency, his incapability of fulfilling his wife's dream and desires. Like his father, he feels apologetic because he cannot do better. He lives with a sense of defeat and failure.

"He understood because, like her, he had been defected too; like her he was a victim. Although each understood the secret truth about the other, it did not bring about any closeness of spirit, any comradeship, because they also sensed that two victims, ought to avoid each other, not yoke together their joint disappointments. A victim does not look to help from another victim, he looks for a redeemer. At least Deven had his poetry, she had nothing, and so there was an added accusation and bitterness in her look" (*IC*, p. 68).

Overtly Deven's trritability and anger at his wife, appears to be the outcome of his hurt male ego. Deep down, his rage is, in a way, an externalization of his self hate. He reproaches himself for his inadequacy to make any distinction in life "..... all he could measure upto was this — this shabby house, its dirty corners, its wretchedness and lovelessness" (*IC*, p. 67). What he had secretly dreamt was "the world of drama and revolving lights and feasts and furies" (*IC*, p. 67) something like Nur's world. The impossibility of translating his dream into reality frustrated him. In society, with friends, he cannot revolt, it is basically alien to his nature. At home he imposes his superiority, turning aggressive and intimidating Sarla. Outside his home he adopts self-minimizing and protective measures. He tries to extricate symapthy from Murad by being apologetic and humble.

Deven who has been living an ordinary mundane life, is suddenly pushed out of this ordinariness, and is given the chance of a lifetime by being asked to interview Nur. The prospect opens up an entirely new world for Deven, a world strange, unfamiliar and over-awing in which he is not quite sure how to conduct himself. Yet a world very different from the one he had expected. The world which opened in front of him, was one of crowded homes, of greedy poets, of the backlanes and brothel houses in Chandini Chowk. There is Nur, the poet and Nur the senile, greedy lustful man. Deven, as he gets to know him is divided between the two Nurs, attracted by one and repelled by the other. In the face of all odds despite humiliation, Deven reaches the poet in all devotion. In fact, Nur the poet represents Deven, all that he has idealized in himself. His image of Nur is hallowed by a dignity and glory which in actuality the poet lacks. "He had pictured him living either surrounded by elderly sages and dignified litertaures or else entirely alone in divine isolation" (*IC*, p. 51). Contrary to this, he meets a senile and debilitated old man presiding over a court of louts and lechers.

Deven has an ambition — to get his monograph published

and to reach somewhere in the literary field but he is not a pushing personality. He often has nightmares, in which he sees himself struggling to reach some destination. Deven's difficulty arises because he lacks self-confidence, he needs a prop to goad him to support him. Luckily for him, help comes from Murad, Siddiqui, Nur's first wife and his students. What he does not realise is that, that each one is out to take advantge of him. Throughout the narrative, Deven feels like a trapped animal. Marriage, family and even his friendship with Nur, appears like a cage. But once when support is withdrawn, he feels betrayed. Deven realises that he has to find his own strength and not depend on others. "Oddly enough, the certainty he could expect no more help from Murad had a calming effect upon him. Perhaps when everyone had cut him off and he was absolutely alone, he would begin to find himself and his own strength" (*IC*, 189-90). Deven explores his own potentialities that he can stand by himself. His strength lies within not without Deven's self discovery at the final moment of crisis is not abrupt, nor is it impossible, although it appears sudden. Deven, according to Usha Bande, suffers from what Maslow terms 'Junah Complex' meaning a tendency to run away from one's best talent... or mission in life. One can get out of this situation with the help of self awareness and self analysis. Deven emerges out of this during his epiphanic moments. He regains his ability to take decision and shoulder his responsibility. He comprehends the secrets of trans-temporal nature of art and literature. Artistic works are not the chracters of social reality, but they transcend it to project the realm of future of possibility. An aesthetic experience enables a perceiver to reach beyond the condition of his existence. Art is an instrument of a liberation; it cannot be expected to offer solutions to problems as science can. Deven's quest ends in value discovery. Understanding of our failing enables us to see glory in all.

After sleepless nights he finally reaches the stage where he can see the perfection of art and imperfection of human nature, reality and illusion all stand clearly illuminated. He is able to separate the two personalities of Nur — the poet and the man. An artist is the child of his age, under the corrupting influence of his time, but his art remains untainted. Deven rejuvenates his vision with the recognition that his friendship with Nur is not a trap but a liberation. He has received the gift of Nur's poetry and "that meant he was custodian of Nur's very soul and spirit. It was a great distinction. He could not deny or abandon that under any pressure" (*IC*, p. 204).

Identified, thus, with the historicity of life he builds a communion of conciousness with Nur and reaches out for an experience of human solidarity and inter-dependence. Deven's temporal experiences are exchanged for the realm of eternal form. He reaches a wholeness of self; achieves the spontaniety when he marches away from a self created trap to the joyous affirmation of life which is a precondition of positive freedom.

In the character of Deven, Anita Desai studies at once a timid and ineffectual but growth-oriented person who shows self-confidence and clarity of vision. Though throughout the novel he is a weak persoanlity, tossed by self effacing drives, all his feebleness is submerged at the crucial moment of self-scrutiny. His awakening typifies coherence and completeness. Deven is not seen as a function of impersonal influences, but it is himself, his character, psychology and action that interests Anita Desai and she invests it with human value and interest. To do this with such dreary, feeble spirit as Deven is evidence of a rare gift for creating something completely authentic and true.

Characters like Deven either live in illusion or show their reluctance to face reality and live in self imposed solitary confinement. To this class, belong Maya, Manisha, Nirode, Raka and Nanda, but there are others who compromise with life. Although they have their problems, they manage to transcend them. Amla suffers existential crisis but soon decides that she will not allow herself to be lost like her sister. Bim accepts the present, linking it with the past to march towards the future. Deven incorporates more dynamic and integrated approach. Desai depicts characters who are deeply sensitive to the grandeur as well as sordidness of life. Desai was neither a visionary nor a mystic but an artist who like, Thomas Hardy, saw the sorriness underlying the grandest things and the grandeur underlying the sorriest things. Her primary concern was not with how one gets along with others but with oneself. The basic problem she felt as how to exist in society, and yet mantain one's individuality. Deven is trapped in his self created mess. Socially he is in a precarious position and suffers humiliation, but finally feels whole despite his challenging experience. The growing urge for self discovery in Desai's character exhibits the growth potential of her protoganist as also the ever developing vision of their creator. Nirode, Sita, Nanda, Sarah, Amla, Bim and Deven indicate a steady progress in their march from self-alienation to self-discovery, from there to self-actualizing, from sickness to health, neurosis to normalcy.

Anita Desai's manifest talent is seen in *In Custody*, it demonstrates the range of her gifts. It is more individual, less generalised and conventional than her earlier fiction. Artistically the work is a great achievement. A subdued stream of humour, irony and sarcasm runs through it, definitely a new dimension in her writing.

The adoration of poetry is at the centre of the thematic, emotional and plot pattern in the novel. Deven's higher artistic aspiration, its fulfilment and consequence form the basis of the study. The climax of the theme comes at the close of the book with Deven yoked in spiritual and material bondage with Nur. The theme is supplemented by a counter balancing of romantic glorification with dissillusionment, admiration with nausea, ideal with real fantasy with truth. *In Custody* like her other novels is a study in higher values — the value of poet and his poetry and the interdependence of critic and the creative artist. The whole undertaking of the interview begins as an adventure but soon becomes a crusade in order to resuscitate not only the dying language but also the dying Nur, and all this is achieved by a meek, self-effacing Deven, who is resigned to his life as a lecturer in an obscure college in the dusty shapeless town of Mirpore. The remarkable skill of Anita Desai has made what seemed to be a story of inevitable tragedy into a tale of triumphant ecstacy.

REFERENCES

1. P.P. Mehta, *Indo-Aglian Fiction — An Assessment.*
2. Srinivas Iyengar, *Indian Writing in English.*
3. M.K. Naik, *Aspects of Indo-Anglian Writing.*
4. William Walsh, *Indian Writing in English.*

5. Usha Bande, *The Novels of Anita Desai.*
6. Jasbir Jain, *Stairs to the Altic.*
7. J.B. Tripati, *The Mind and Art of Anita Desai.*
8. Anita Desai, *In Custody*, Penguin (1984).

13

The Conflict between Imperialism and Nationalism in *I Shall Not Hear the Nightingale*

—Dr. Basavaraj Naikar

THE conflict between the colonizer and the colonized happens to be a major thematic concern in many Indian English novels like R.K.Narayan's *Waiting for the Mahatma*, Raja Rao's *Kanthapura*, Malgaonkar's *A Bend in the Ganges*, Chaman Nahal's *Azadi* and Khushwant Singh's *I Shall Not Hear the Nightingale* (1959). In these novels different aspects of colonial encounter between Indians and Britishers like protest, submission, love-hate relationship, compromise etc. are highlighted and are, therefore, comparable to similar novels by Commonwealth writers like Chinua Achebe, Ngugi and Patrick White and so on.

In *I Shall Not Hear the Nightingale*, Khushwant Singh presents the colonial encounter between Indians and the British Government against the background of the Punjab. Punjab, the land of five rivers is known for its own distinctive geographical features, its military history and Sikh religion which easily set it off from the other ethnic cultures of India, although it belongs to India politically. Khushwant Singh has tried to give a very microscopic picture of the Punjabi life in the novel even when he concentrates his attention on the political theme.

The novel deals with the India of 1940s, when the colonial encounter between the Indians and the British was moving towards a climax on account of the emergence of nationalistic consciousness among the Indians. There had always been a mixed reaction among Indians towards the British Raj. Khushwant Singh presents a microscopic picture of the strange mixture of attitudes to the alien rule through the depiction of life in Amritsar district. The situation presented here is easily comparable to those in other colonized countries like Africa and West Indies etc.

The characters in *I Shall Not Hear the Nightingale* can be broadly classified into two groups : one, Sardar Buta Singh, Wazir Chand, John Taylor and Lambardar are pro-British in their attitude; two : Sher Singh, Madan and other student leaders are anti-British in their attitude. The central irony in the novel is evident in the fact that both the pro-British and the anti-British ideologies are cherished by different members of the same family. (This situation provides a very good contrast to the one depicted in Chinua Achebe's *Things Fall Apart.*) Buta Singh, for example, happens to be a District Magistrate who has a great admiration for the British rule in India. "...loyalty to the Raj had been as much an article of faith with him as it had been with his father and grandfather who had served in the army. He, like them, had mentioned the English king or queen in his evening prayer, O, Guru, bless our Sovereign and bless us their subjects so that we remain contented and happy" (p. 23). Buta Singh tells his son that "the Indians should help the British in their war against the Germans and other European powers. I do believe that in this war our interests and that of the English are identical. If they lose, we lose. If we help them to win, they will certainly give us something more than we have now. We should know who are our friends and who are our enemies. The English have ruled us for over a hundred years, and I don't care what you say. I believe they have treated us better than our own kings did in the past; or the Germans, Italians, or Japanese will do if they win and take our India. We must stand by the English in their hour of trouble" (p. 23).

Buta Singh knows that his sympathy for the British rule in India may earn him the scorn of his own countrymen. But he does not mind being unpopular with his countrymen as long as he has the patronage of the British rulers like, for example, the District Commissioner, Mr. John Taylor. Bata Singh's attitude to life is opportunistic in that he wants to accept the contingencies of political life and turn them to his own best possible advantage so that he can lead a life of security and ensure happiness for his family.

Buta Singh's son Sher Singh believes in a diametrically opposite philosophy of life. A young and energetic student in the local college, he heads the Student Union as its President. He is not very serious about his studies, but he is fired by the patriotic zeal and nationalistic philosophy popularized by Mahatma Gandhi, Nehru and other leaders. He questions the very rationale of the British rule in India and pleads for self-government for the motherland. He is not influenced by his father's loyalty to the British. He, therefore, reacts very strongly to his father, "We are far too concerned with other people. Our Communist friends are only worried about what will happen to Russia; others think only of what will happen to Britain. Very few of us are bothered with our own future" (p. 23). Sher Singh is, thus, deeply concerned with the Indian life. He becomes an embodiment of the nationalistic ideal. He enjoys the support of a large mass of students and consequently conducts several secret meetings of students thereby planning to carry out terroristic activities in the city of Amritsar. He has the cooperation of other leaders like Madan, son of Wazir Chand. Thus the conflict between the pro-British attitude and the anti-British comes into operation in one and the same family which may be said to be a microscopic symbol of the macroscopic phenomenon of the Indian political life.

The womenfolk of Buta Singh's family or of Wazir Chand's family are not bothered about the political life of the country. They are mainly concerned with the security of family life and comfortable living. Sabhrai, wife of Buta Singh, for example, happens to be a very religious lady who believes in the sanctity of *Granth Sahib* and supremacy of Guru Govind Singh. She believes that what her husband does is right and that her son Sher Singh should not be cross with his father. Likewise, Sher Singh's young wife Champak is also not bothered about his public life and nationalistic and terroristic activities. She is very keen on the enjoyment of regular matrimonial sex and even commits adultery with Madan secretly. The sisters of Sher Singh and Madan are concerned only with their studies. But all of them tacitly agree with their parental sympathy for the British rule in India.

Buta Singh's sympathy for the British rule is supported by his knowledge of the internal contradictions and conflicts of Indian life. He knows that there is no homogeneous society in India and that it is a mosaic of many castes and cultures, like the Sikh, the Hindu and the Muslim among others. He knows that the ethnic conflicts are sparked off in the country at the slightest provocation and result in violence and chaos. He, therefore, believes that the British rule can keep these violent and conflicting forces under check and offer a political unity to India.

The conflict between the pro-British and the anti-British continues all through the novel. Sher Singh expresses his nationalistic ideology in the fiery speech he delivers at the gathering of patriotic students, "Comrades, we meet at a crucial time. The enemy is at our gates... Comrades, we not only have the enemy at our door step, we have enemies within our own house ... Those who sacrifice the interests of the motherland for foreign countries are our enemy No. l. They have been rightly named as the *Kaum nashts* — destroyers of the race ... There are also people who want to cut off the limbs of Mother India and make another state of Pakistan. They too are our enemies ... But we are Sikhs who do not fear any enemies. We shall destroy all those who stand in our way" (p. 39). His patriotic speech whips up the nationalistic zeal in the audience and elicits a great applause from them.

Buta Singh does not encourage his son to indulge in anti-British activities. Though he knows the general trend of his son's thinking, he does not know any details of his secret activities. He enjoys the confidence of the D.C. John Taylor and offers his suggestions to the latter in solving some of the local problems. When, for example, John Taylor issues an order banning the Hindu procession in the city, the Hindus feel insulted and irritated because the Muslim and Sikh processions were not banned earlier. Wazir Chand who is a Hindu wants to meet the D.C. and get permission for the Hindu procession by explaining the situation. But he is not permitted by the District Commissioner. He, therefore, seeks the help of Buta Singh and requests him to explain the sensitiveness of the communal issue to John Taylor and get at least a relaxation of the ban order. Buta Singh who enjoys the confidence of John Taylor meets the latter at his residence, explains the possibility of communal explosion in the city and finally but gently persuades him to relax the ban order against the Hindu procession at least for a few hours. Wazir Chand and his friends thank Buta Singh for helping them.

The ideological conflict between father and son continues all through the novel. When Buta Singh habitually admires the British people and their impartiality etc., and suggests that "We Indians have a lot to learn from them," Sher Singh boldly crosses his father and argues that the British "too have something to learn from us ... like hospitality ... tolerance ... etc." (p. 77). Buta Singh pinpoints the mutual intolerance among Hindus, Sikhs and Muslims and highlights the so-called impartiality and tolerance of the British people. Sher Singh does not hesitate to show the racial discrimination practised by the British elsewhere, "You can find examples like that everywhere. Most white people are anti-Semitic. It's not only Hitler who has been putting Jews in gas chambers, the Russians have killed many. Everywhere in Europe and America there is prejudice against them and only because they have better brains and talent than others. We do not have any racial discrimination" (p. 77). Sher Singh's mother Sabhrai does not like his being cross with his father and asks him, "Tell me, son, what will you get if the English leave this country?" (p. 78). Then Sher Singh replies that the country will be free. He waxes lyrical and hopes that "Spring will come to our barren land once more ... once more the nightingales will sing" (p. 79). The song of nightingales thus becomes a symbol of freedom and joy for Sher Singh.

Meanwhile, the members of Buta Singh's family grow closer to those of Wazir Chand's family. Buta Singh's daughter, Beena and daughter-in-law, Champak join Wazir Chand's son Madan Lal and daughter Sita and all together go to Simla to spend some time in summer. The ideological similarity between Sher Singh and Madan Lal has, obviously, brought the two families closer. Madan Lal who, in spite of being a nationalist, is an unfailing seducer of women. On account of his physical handsomeness, sophisticated manners and abundant chivalry, he succeeds in tempting and finally seducing Champak thereby creating a sexual jealousy between Beena and Champak. Even when Sabhrai joins tham in Simla to prevent the possible damage to Beena's virginity or

Champak's chastity, she is very cleverly fooled by Madan Lal, who shows her extraordinary respect and courtesy and silences her suspicion about the violation of the family's sexual morals.

Meanwhile, Sher Singh associates himself with the terrorists of Amritsar and begins to indulge in the terroristic activities in the city. He is so much preoccupied with the nationalistic-cum-terroristic activities that he remains blissfully ignorant about the loss of his wife's chastity. In spite of his knowledge about Madan Lal's being a notorious womanizer, he fails to know that he has been cuckolded by the latter. Though Sher Singh hates the British rule and the British officers, he is persuaded by his father to meet the District Ccmmissioner Mr. John Taylor to develop some familiarity with him and consequently to change his attitude towards him. Buta Singh expresses his pure admiration for the British people, "As I was saying, these Englishmen take a lot of interest in other people, and it is not just curiosity, it is a genuine concern with their problems. Now Taylor knows all of you by name, what you are doing, how you have fared in your examinations everything. He has an excellent memory" (p. 94). Far from being impressed by his father's Anglophilia, Sher Singh offers his severe comment on the Englishmen, "They have learnt from Americans ... They have reduced human relationships to a set of rules. They say you must know the name of the person you are talking to and use it as often as possible. You must know his or her interest and talk about them and never of your own. They write down whatever they have discussed with anyone in their diaries and refresh their memories before the next meeting. It does not mean much because their real desire is to create a good impression about themselves. They are not one bit concerned with the affairs of the person they happen to be talking to" (p. 94). In spite of Sher Singh's strong dislike for the Englishmen, he yields to parental persuasion and wifely order and meets John Taylor by way of courtesy.

But when he meets John Taylor much against his willingness, he feels angry with himself. Although Taylor treats him with courtesy and advises him to relax in the summer holidays at Shimla and even offers him permission to own a rifle, Sher Singh feels confused between the contradictory feelings in himself like respecting the authority of the District Commissioner on the one hand and his hatred for the British rule on the other. Similarly he feels confused between his fear of the empty cartridges fingered by John Taylor and his eagerness to drive out the British from India. He feels a sense of humiliation at having agreed to meet John Taylor and a sense of anger at his parents and wife for having pressurized him, to meet the officer. He, therefore, returns home with a decision never to repeat such a compromising act.

Sher Singh dreams of harmonizing the contradictory philosophies of his family somehow or the other, without realizing the impossibility of such a happening in real life, *i.e.*, in 1942 in India. "Britain had to get out of India herself or be kicked out, and Sher Singh would say that to Taylor's face. Could he? What about his father's views? his cousin in service and his hope of finding his name in the next Honours list? And the-unique honour he was getting in the way of an armed police guard outside his house — the sentry who sprang to attention and smacked the butt of his rifle even when Sher Singh passed by with his college friends? Couldn't it somehow happen that these opposite factors could be combined into one harmonious whole? He visualized scenes when his Nationalist and terrorist colleagues honoured him as their beloved leader, where Taylor read an address of welcome and his father proudly looked on. Such were the dreams with which Sher Singh tried to dope himself. They were based on the non-discovery of one party by the other" (p. 118). Thus Sher Singh dreams of achieving his ideal and hope to concretise his plans by resolving the confusion in his mind.

As his will power grows stronger with the passing of time, he decides to resort to terroristic action. He, therefore, calls a secret meeting of his student friends near the canal bridge outside the city. He hides the arms in his garage to escape the notice of the Government police. He also knows that some of his fellow conspirators might be informers against him and therefore remains quite alert.

One day the village headman, Lambardarji, meets Sher Singh at his home and pretends to be very friendly with him. Sher Singh treats him with buttermilk. The village headman cleverly tries to elicit some information about the Hindu boys who participated in the shooting party few days ago. Then Sher Singh begins to suspect that the village headmen may not be really as innocent as he appears, in spite of his courteous behaviour and fine manners. Suspecting him to be an informant to John Taylor, Sher Singh offers him some money as a gift, though inwardly he knows he has given it to him as 'blackmail money.' He also knows that he may have to give more money to the village headman to keep his secrets concealed by the Government.

By this time, the nationalist activities begin rigorously in north India under the influence of Mahatma Gandhi. The Gandhi-cap covered patriots begin to attack the shops and public offices. The British soldiers try to beat the patriots violently. Thus, the nationalistic struggle gathers force and occupies the mind of Indians who tend to forget or neglect their personal problems. Shops are looted, roads are blocked and trains are stopped by the nationalist agitators. Sher Singh reads the newspapers full of news about the nation-wide agitation. He also receives a cyclostyled letter with a caption, 'A Manifesto of the Hindustan Socialist Republican Army.' "It drew attention to the arrests of the leaders and asked the youth of India to arise and rid themselves of foreign rule. it did not mince its words, Shoot English officials and the Indian toadies who serve them. Destroy roads and bridges; cut telegraph and telephcne wires; create chaos and paralyse the administration. This is your sacred duty. Long live the revolution" (p. 151).

After learning about the spread of nationalistic movement all over the country, Sher Singh's rebellious impulse grows more and more intense. Finally he overcomes his confusion and oscillation and decides to indulge in terroristic action. He, therefore, calls a secret meeting of his fellow rebels and takes the oath of liberating the country from the foreign rule. They take the oath of secrecy before indulging in terroristic action. They are inspired by Mahatma Gandhi in general and by Bhagat Singh in particular. They define their terroristic targets clearly. As Sher Singh makes it clear, "The call is to destroy means of communication. A few bridges blown up, a few roads barricaded and the British Army will be stuck where it is" (p. 153). Accordingly, they take six hand grenades and initially blow the central bridge and think that nobody knows about themselves.

Since the nationalistic activities spread all over the country, the British officers, especially John Taylor become very alert and try to control the situation as far as they can. John Taylor, therefore, sends for Buta Singh to track down the agitators unofficially. He also suggests to Buta Singh that he knows about Sher Singh's nationalistic activities. He explains to him clearly that they would leave India as soon as the war is over. "Your son could do a good service to his friends and his country. You know we are anxious to get out of India and hand over the reins of power to you people as soon as the war is won. But we will not leave the country to the Japanese or the Germans. And these acts are calculated to do just that — hand over India on a silver platter to the Fascist powers" (p. 159). An ardent admirer of British rule, Buta Singh decides to advise his son at his leisure.

Meanwhile, the village headman, Lambardar meets Sher Singh at home and asks for compensation of Rs. 300 for the medical treatment of his bullock which has broken its leg in the holes created by the grenades in the canal. Sher Singh treats him nicely by giving him buttered toast and asks him to see him at the canal bridge in the evening. Sher Singh inwardly suspects that Lambardar being an informer to the British Government, was trying to exploit the situation. When Lambardar sees Sher Singh and his friends including Madan Lal near the canal bridge, there is an exchange of hot words between them. Lambardar's behaviour changes from the modest to the arrogant. Sher Singh and his friends like, Madan, grow certain about his being an informer to the Government and therefore, Sher Singh shoots him to death. Lambardar sags to the earth cursing them, "I'll sleep with your mothers ... I'll sleep with your sisters ... I'll..." (p. 168). Immediately they bury the deadbody and disperse from there.

After the death of Lambardar, his son Jimma Singh is appointed as the village headman and is given a revolver to defend himself. Jimma Singh has three wives and yet he has no single progeny. One day he disappears from the village for three days without telling anyone of his wives. The disappearance of Jimma Singh is attributed to his murder by one of his relatives. The same is reported to the Police Commissioner who sends the file to the Deputy Commissioner to have the case closed as 'untraced'. But the Deputy Commissioner sends a warrant to search the house of Sardar Buta Singh, the seniormost Indian Magistrate of the district and another one to arrest Sher Singh. John Taylor wants to treat Buta Singh gently and therefore sends for him. When Buta Singh meets John Taylor at home, his house is searched by the Police Commissioner. The police constables beat Sher Singh, Mundoo and the dog called Dyer. They arrest Sher Singh and take him to prison. Champak is simply flabbergasted by the sight of what has happened to her husband and family. Buta Singh does not know what is happening in his house in his absence. He narrates the history of the loyalty of his family to the British Crown right from the days of Sikh rule. "Sir, we can almost go back to the days of Sikh rule. On the annexation of the Punjab and the disbanding of Sikh forces, my great grandfather, who was a *subedar* and had fought against the British in the Anglo-Sikh wars, joined the British army. He served, under John Lawrence. He also fought under Nicholson in the Mutiny of 1857 and was awarded a medal for the capture of Delhi; we still have it in the family. My grandfather was also in the British army. He rose from the rant and retired as a Jamedar — in those days to be a Jamedar was a big thing for an Indian. My father did not join the army, but he recruited many soldiers in the 1914-18 war and our family was given lands in the Canal Colonies. I have kept up the tradition of loyalty to the British Crown and will do so till the day I die" (p. 180). Although Buta Singh expresses his loyalty to the British Crown, John Taylor knows that the British are going to leave India in the near future. He, therefore, says to Buta Singh, "I appreciate your sentiments of loyalty, Buta Singh, but I do not agree with you about the future of India; and I am British. I feel we should pull out of this country as soon after the war as we can and let you Indians manage your own affairs. 1, for one, have no intention of continuing in the Indian Civil Service a day after the cease fire. In fact I am not on the side of Mr.Churchill but on that of Mr. Gandhi and Mr. Nehru — except, and this is important, I do think the war has to be won first. Otherwise the Nazis and the Fascists will put the clock back for you and for us. I may be wrong, but that is my belief" (p. 180). Then John Taylor gently asks Buta Singh about his son's nationalistic and terroristic activities and his possible connection with the murder of the village headman, Jimma Singh. Buta Singh is simply shocked out of his wits and begins to cry for shame. He covers his face with his palms and blurts out, "My nose has been cut. I can no longer show my face to the world" (p. 182). John Taylor tells him further that his son Sher Singh has been put into jail and gives him fifteen days leave and allows him to see and advise his son as often as he can.

On receiving a telegram from Buta Singh, Sabhrai and Beena return from Shimla by train and are unexpectedly received in the Railway Station by Mrs. Joyce Taylor and dropped at her home. Buta Singh explains to his wife how their son has been sent to jail for his being connected with terroristic activities and murder of the village headman. Champak also feels crestfallen. Sabhrai is totally confounded by her son's behaviour. Although she does not fully understand the implications of her son's activities, she wants to have her piece of the moon back at home. Her emotional attachment for her husband as well as her son makes her not to bother too much about political ideologies. A lady of deep religious bent of mind, she believes in the spiritual powers of Guru Govind Singh and the holy *Granth*.

Buta Singh with his pro-British attitude is so much angered and insulted by his son's arrest that he refuses to go to the prison to talk to Sher Singh. Likewise, Sher Singh also knows that his father does not spare him in case he visits him in the prison. When Sher Singh's parents-in-law hear about his imprisonment, they take away their daughter Champak back to their place.

Meanwhile, Sher Singh is interrogated by the Sahibs. But Sher Singh wants to consult his father or a lawyer before that. Finally he is allowed to consult his father. But since Buta Singh flatly refuses to see him in prison, his wife Sabhrai wants to see him after four days.

Buta Singh fears that his son's anti-British activities may cost him his own job, pension and other amenities of life which he owes to the British sympathy. Feeling terribly insecure in life, he grows unusually religious and reads the holy *Granth*. Sabhari spends a whole night in the golden temple bathing in the cold water and meditating and praying all through the night. She waits for the spiritual guidance from the Guru in the present crisis. The next day she visits her son in the prison, gives him the holy dust from the temple and advises him not to name the other culprits. She knows that Sher Singh has done wrong but she invokes the Guru to guide him.

After returning from the prison, Mrs Sabhrai sends a letter thanking Mrs. Taylor for all the kindness shown to her. The letter is full of filial tenderness and touches the heart of the addressee. "Dear Taylor Memsahib, I am an uneducated Punjabi woman who cannot write nice words of thanks in English. Ask one of your clerks to read this to you. God bless you for what you have done. You wanted to share the grief of a mother whose child has been stricken. There is no greater act of kindness in this world. May the Guru's blessings be on you, your Sahib and on your children. May you have many sons. May God ever keep your household full of plenty and keep sorrow and suffering away from your door" (p. 211). Sabhrai sends the letter with the chauffeur to Joyce Taylor. Then she is down with fever and pneumonia.

Buta Singh thinks that only the Englishman *i.e.,* John Taylor can help him out of the crisis. He wants to please the Englishman with some Christmas gifts. He, therefore, arranges to send some fine oranges to John Taylor and his wife and a finely composed letter in the name of his wife which shows their admiration for the British authorities. It reads as follows :

Respected Mrs.Taylor,

Pray accept this humble gift of oranges for Christmas Day. They are the first pick of the year from our garden. I hope you will like them. To you and to your noble husband and children our most respected Deputy Commissioner, my husband and children owe their all. Madam will do us an honour by receiving this very little gift on the auspecious occasion of the birthday of the world Saviour, Lord Jesus Christ.

Your humble servant
Sabhrai
(Sardarini Buta Singh) wife of
Sardar Buta Singh, B.A. (Hons)
Magistrate, First Class (p. 214).

The Christmas gift of oranges is luckily received by Joyce Taylor who shows the humanitarian courtesy by visiting Sabhrai. Joyce Taylor, who was trained as a nurse before marrying John Taylor, examines the health of Sabhrai. Sabhrai is in delirium and cannot speak but she shows her gratitude to Joyce Taylor by the quivering movement of her lips. Joyce Taylor tries to enhearten Sabhrai and her husband and daughter. She knows that Sabhrai is suffering from pneumonia. She is so much touched by the plight of a religious mother *i.e.,* Sabhrai that she persuades her husband John Taylor to give a real Christmas gift to Buta Singh's family in the form of release of Sher Singh on the Christmas Day itself. John Taylor knows that he has ordered the arrest of Sher Singh on mere suspicion without having any solid proof about the murder of the village headman. His knowledge about Buta Singh's firm loyalty to the British, Sabhrai's religious bent of mind and physical suffering and his wife's pressure, finally compel him to order for the release of Sher Singh on the Christmas Day. Sher Singh is ecstatic about his release when he is taken out of the prison into the city in a procession by his friends and nationalist zealots. Thus, Sher Singh becomes a hero in the eyes of his fellow rebels and nationalists. He is garlanded, photographed and cheered by the enthusiastic audience. He thumps his chest and declares, "Comrades ... I'will cherish the honor you have done me today for the rest of my life. I am proved that I was called upon to do a small duty to my country and I did it ... You all know how well the King Emperor — may peace be upon him — looks after his guests ... But they could not break the spirit of the son of India and God willing they will never will" (p. 224-25). Obviously, Sher Singh's father, mother, sister and wife are very happy about his release. Sabhrai recovers her health temporarily and spends some happy moments with the members of her family. The doctors opine that she should not be allowed to be excited. The release of Sher Singh is followed by another happy event *i.e.*, the declaration of O.B.E. title for Buta Singh in the New Year's Honour's list. Buta Singh initially refuses to believe it, but when the newspaper correspondents, colleagues and friends come to garland and congratulate him, he accepts it as real. Everybody in the family is very happy.

But alas, the happiness does not continue for long because Sabhrai, after four days' cheerfulness, begins to sink suddenly. She knows that she is going to die and says, "My time has come" (p. 231). She sends for all the members of her family and makes them read the holy *Granth*. Then she dies while uttering the prayer. Her funeral is conducted with due honour and dignity. The Taylors and many officials send wreaths as a mark of their respect for the late Sabhrai.

Buta Singh's loyalty to the British Crown has earned him the right kind of reward. He, therefore, wants to thank Mr. John Taylor for the O.B.E. title and for his releasing his son so quickly and unexpectedly and Mrs. Joyce Taylor for her kindness shown to his family. He also wants to seek the help of John Taylor in fixing a job for his son. He wants to build a memorial for his late wife Sabhrai in consultation with the Taylors. He buys a new tie and wears it before meeting them and thanks them profusely and consults them about his son's job and a memorial for his late wife. The Taylors treat him with great courtesy and friendliness so much so that Buta Singh feels that he is one of their family friends. Thus the novel *I Shall Not Hear the Nightingale* delineates the paradoxical picture of the colonial encounter between the Indians and the British including both the positive and the negative aspects, the submission as well as rebellion simultaneously involved in it. As already pointed out earlier, this novel can be easily contrasted with Chinua Achebe's *Things Fall Apart* where the same theme is depicted in a reverse fashion. Whereas in *I Shall Not Hear The Nightingale*, the son rebels against the British rule and the father submits to it, in *Things Fall Apart*, the father rebels against the British rule and the son submits to it in the form of being converted to Christianity.

Apart from the colonial conflict depicted in *I Shall Not Hear The Nightingale*, there are other details in the novel which are very realistic and interesting. Khushwant Singh is known for his stark realism and evocation of the Indian, especially the Sikh culture in the novel. He is not a puritanical writer who sugercoats the truth of life. On the contrary, he is a realist and modernist in the sense that he has the courage to look into the face of harsh reality and and describe it precisely and objectively without any sentimentalism or exaggeration. For example, apart from the depiction of Buta Singh's admiration for the British rule, Sher Singh's antipathy for the same and Sabhrai's religious nature, Khushwant Singh offers a very realistic picture of Champak's sexuality, like her shaving of pubic hair, Mundoo's juvenile curiosity about feminine nakedness, Shunno's anal bleeding and her sexual surrender to the Peer Sahib, Madan's shameless womanization etc., without any hypocritical slurring over them. In this sense, Khushwant Singh can be easily compared to Mulk Raj Anand, Chinua Achebe, Ngugi va Thiang'O and other Commonwealth novelists.

NOTE

All the page references are to *I Shall Not Hear The Nightingale*, by Khushwant Singh, IBH Publishing Company, Bombay, 1973.

14

Fantasy in Arun Joshi's *The City and The River*

—Dr. Ashok Kumar Bachchan

THE City and the River (1990) is 'a mixture of fantasy, prophecy, and a startlingly real vision of everyday politics, ... that is truly a parable of the times.'[1] In his earlier novels as well Arun Joshi had been interested in the mode of fantasy and satire especially in *The Strange Case of Billy Biswas* and *The Apprentice.* But whereas in the previous novels fantasy and satire had been incidental, in *The City and the River* these constitute the basic fictional technique.

The City and the River is the only fictional work by Arun Joshi bearing a title conjoined by the cumulative conjunction 'and.' This serves to juxtapose the first noun phrase 'the city' with the second 'the river.' Both these are inanimate objects which have been used as symbols of the two ways of life. The City represents the city state governed by the Grand Master, who runs it with the assistance of a Council of Advisors. The river passing by the city symbolizes the endless flow of life. The real sons of rivers are the boatmen living in mud-houses that lie scattered by the river on the outskirts of the city. The city had its elite living in 'the neat rosy pink, oval of the brick colonies.'[2]

The brick-people have all lost their authenticity and are not concerned with what goes on in their city state. The mud-people, on the other hand, are all deeply involved in the anti-repressive measures adopted to subjugate them. The Grand Master with his advisors creates a reign of terror and the state terrorism is let loose. The Grand Master assisted by his son and advisors use the latest scientific equipment to suppress boatmen's rebellion. Boatmen are tortured, their headperson, who is a woman, is imprisoned and blinded. There is much destruction of life and property including the Grand-father's Rose farm and the inmates on it. Finally, nature has its own revenge as the river rises to an unprecedented level and washes away the entire city including its buildings and inmates, leaving no traces of any habitation. Yet, out of the ruins of the old city a new one rises up; and it has all the ways of life that had been there in the old city. Out of the flood only one person survives, and he has been simply called nameless-one, who is an illegal child and who is sent to the city with the mission to re-establish it.

The novel opens with *Prologue* and ends with *Epilogue.* In between the two it has nine chapters narrating the rule of the Grand Master, his becoming king, the perpetuation of the reign of terror, people's rebellion, the declaration of an Era of Ultimate Greatness, which is tentamount to the clamping of the rule of Emergency, the repressive measures adopted by the king, and lastly, the destruction of the city with the great flood.

Prologue and *Epilogue* inform us of the narrative strategy of the novel. The great Yogeshwar is an ageless seer and teacher at whose feet several persons of the novel such as Astrologer, the Minister for Trade and the Hermit of the Mountain have also received education. The agelessness of the teacher is borne up by the fact that 'a hundred years ago, as young students, the Astrologer and the Hermit had long debated this particular parallelogram.'[3] Both of the disciples have crossed much more than a century of their lives and their teacher, the great Yogeshwar, must have been almost ageless. The *Prologue* tells us about the last day of Nameless — one with the great Yogeshwar. The great Yogeshwar celebrates his pupil's thirtieth birthday by revealing to him who he is. Moreover, he points out to him 'the mystery of the world and how to keep the grain and the chaff apart.'[4] The great Yogeshwar also teaches him the secret of the body and that of the spirit and how the spirit gained the control of the body. He also teaches his pupil the way of the pilgrim and the way of the warrior, cautions him about 'the ways of the tyrant'[5] and how to wait. The Great Yogeshwar teaches him everything but tells him nothing about who he is. The Great

Yogeshwar reads out something from a book of yellowed sheets, containing 'a strange, sorry tale.'[6] To celebrate his thirtieth birthday the teacher offers him elixir which is 'the colour of the peacock's feathers.'[7] It makes the Nameless-one aware of the music and the dance prevailing in the infinite spaces of the cosmic night and he feels 'as vast as the sky and as tall as the mountain.'[8] The teacher is satisfied that his disciple also sees the dancing of a God and then he tells him :

> I shall tell you now a tale and in my telling, perhaps, you will know who you are. Listen, this is how it goes.[9]

Then follows the narrative of the novel in about two hundred and fifty pages describing the city and the river. This is crowned by *Epilogue* beginning with the question posed by the Nameless-one 'and then what happened.'[10] The Great Yogeshwar then goes on to tell him of the fate of the periodic disintegration and regeneration of the city and its different activities. All this has happened thirty years ago when the Nameless-one, an illegal child, had been placed on a raft floating on the river. The Great Yogeshwar himself comes by him and not only rears him up but also educates him. In *Epilogue,* the Great Yogeshwar sends him back to the city in the same raft which had taken him to the Great Yogeshwar. The Great Yogeshwar tells the Nameless-one of the endless repetition and periodic disintegration and sends him back to the city 'to prevent this endless repetition, this periodic disintegration'[11] but cautions him that 'to achieve that we need purity.'[12] The sage means thereby that he should purify himself 'of egoism, selfishness stupidity.'[13] Its acquisition is a question of trying 'but purety can come only through sacrifice.'[14] By way of telling him who he is, the Great Yogeshwar teaches him that 'God resides as much in a Grand Master as in you and me.'[15] The sage tells him, moreover, 'it is what you are inside that governs how you read outside.'[16] The sage also promises to him that he would be with him as an instrument 'of the great God in the highest heaven who is the master of the universe.'[17] The Nameless-one in his journey to the city finds a casket of burnished brass containing within a prophesy which had also been there with the previous city and which had been a topic of much debate by the great Yogeshwar's former disciples. Regarding the fate of the city the Great Yogeshwar elaborates :

> On the ruins of that city as always happens, a new city has risen. It is ruled by another Grand Master, which, of course, need not always happen. In the new city is another Professor, another Bhumiputra, another tribe of boatmen. There is also another council and another set of councillors. The men have other names but the forces they embody remain unchanged. And into all this when you go you will, perhaps, be known as another hermit of the Mountain. And it is possible you will have a disciple whose name will be Little Star. To someone this replay, this repetition of things, might appear as a charade, a joke. But, then, whoever said the good Lord did not have humour.[18]

Prologue and *Epilogue* bring out the cyclic motion of the novel. As Usha Bande says, 'the story ends where it begins and begins where it ends.'[19] She rightly compares it with T.S. Eliot's lines in *The Four Quartets :*

> In my beginning is my end. In succession.
> Houses rise and fall, crumble, are extended,
> Are removed, destroyed, restored.[20]

Prologue and *Epilogue* tell nothing palpable or concerete about the narrative but these prepare us for the interpretation of the novel as a whole. The paragraph quoted from the text is related to the continuation of 'the psychic march of humanity'[21] in which 'a new city is reborn like the phoenix on the ruins of the old.'[22]

Prologue and *Epilogue* read like extracts from some allegory or parable. Arun Joshi's interests in these have shifted from the narration of the personal crisis to that of the public. Yet as individuals make up the public, the questions of the crisis of individual identity are not far-off. This is amply illustrated from the reference to 'the strange sorry tale'[23] which is about that of the destruction of the city. The great Yogeshwar points out to his disciple — the Nameless-one — the importance of the recurring problems in the cycle of regeneration and decay, concerning a matter of 'allegiance to God or to man.'[24] This statement makes the novel hinge upon the problems of both religion (God) and politics (man). *Prologue* and *Epilogue* have certain deeper associations as well. These are associated with certain mythical archetypes. G.S. Amur associates the escape of the Nameless-one from the deluge with 'Shishumara of the Indian myths.'[25] There are, moreover, many other archetypal patterns in these episodes. Usha Bande has drawn our attention to it. The Great Yogeshwar is Purana Purusha and the Nameless-one is symbolic of the Manu on the raft on the day of the *Pralaya* saving the Vedas. The Great Yogeshwar is also like Lord Krishna, telling his disciple the gospel of duty and making him feel as vast as the sky and as tall as the mountains. The Nameless-one is also a Christ-figure. He is an illegal child but a chosen one.

With this background of *Prologue* and *Epilogue* we move forward to an analysis of the technique of fantasy in *The City and the River. The City and the River* follows the technique of fantasy which E.M. Forster treats to be one of the aspects of the novel. But in the *Aspects of the Novel,* Forster has not defined fantasy in very clear and definite terms. He goes on to describe fantasy in a rather metaphorical way. It has along with prophesy the 'sense of mythology.'[26] But it is not that the mythologies adopted by fantasy and prophesy are the same. Forster tells us, moreover, 'by their mythologies we shall distinguish these two sorts of novel's.'[27] Fantasy, says Forster, 'implies the Supernatural, but need not express it.'[28] Referring to Sterne's *Tristram Shandy,* a work of fantasy, Forster says that the name of God hidden in it is 'Muddle.'[29] while commenting on *Flecker's Magic* Forster calls its author, Norman Matson, 'a true fantasist'[30] who 'merges the kingdoms of magic and common sense by using words that apply to both.'[31] Herein Forster comes to a kind of definition of fantasy. But much more appropriate than this definition is the description of fantasy in an essay on *Erewhon* as *A Book That Influenced Me* :

> I like that idea of fantasy, of muddling up the actual and the impossible until the reader isn't sure which is which, and I have sometimes tried to do it when writing myself.[32]

This technique of muddling up the actual and the impossible is dominant one in Arun Joshi's *The City and the River*. To understand its mechanism it will be useful if we quote in full. Forster's cataloguing of the devices :

> which writers of a fantastic turn have used — such as the introduction of a god, ghost, angel, monkey, monster, midget, witch into ordinary life; or the introduction of ordinary men into no man's land, the future, the past, the interior of the earth, the fourth dimension, or divings into and dividings of personality, or finally the device of parody or adaptation.[33]

The City and the River is a work of fantasy on the model of the above description. There are in it the descriptions of the supernatural that provides it with the atmosphere of make-believe. There is a deliberate mixture in *The City and the River* of the real and the imaginary. Arun Joshi takes his characters into no man's land, the past as well as the future. The device of parody or adaptations of life and literature are also definitely here in it. Arun Joshi also studies his characters in which he is concerned with the divings into and dividings of personality. In the life of the Professor even the stars have their say. One of his little disciples that materialises from the sky is called the Little Star who had once been called Patanjali. The Little Star quotes that he is 'thousands of years old.'[34] The raft sailing on the river has also on element of fantasy. It has no oars and no boatmen but it sails on with the tune of music. Master Bhoma's disappearance is held up to be a mystery because 'this man simply disappeared between his house and the first lock-up.'[35] This incident generates lots of fuss. The truth was that master Bhoma had simply walked away when the jeep carrying him struck against a pole.

There are several other fantastic references in *The City and the River*. It is said about the Police Commissioner that he had 'developed a machine for examining people's ears and determining the extent of contamination,'[36] This makes a travesty of Draconian regulations which banned even the listening to criticism against the government. Bhoma's parable of the weaving of the invisible clothing for the king and the king's putting it on in a special festival are also effective constituents of fantasy. Everyone sees that the astrologer wove no fabric and that the king put on no robes, yet nobody, except a child, dare comment that the king is naked. In this Arun Joshi makes a travesty of the Era of Ultimate Greatness which admits of no dissent.

Dharma's father, standing before a mirror, sees that his 'insides are rotting.'[37] Even the doctor advises him to 'exercise your soul. Take it for walks.'[38] The scroll containing the city's horoscope has also muddling up of the actual and the impossible. There is much debate regarding the interpretation of the illogicality of 'the river, I see, from a teacher rise' :

> A hundred years ago, as young students, the Astrologer and the Hermit had long debated this particular parallelogram. Their dispute had centred on a single line. Where the Hermit read 'The river, I see, from a teacher rise', the Astrologer maintained "A teacher, I see, from the river rise."
>
> They had disputed that line endlessly. They had sought their teacher's interpretation, but the Great Yogeshwar had merely smiled. Finally, one day he had said, 'cities, my children, even as men, make their own horoscopes'. They had pressed him for more but that was all that he would say.[39]

The mode of fantasy is not very new to Arun Joshi in *The City and the River*. The elements of fantasy are also there in *The Strange Case of Billy Biswas,* but *The City and the River* develops this mode rather consistently from the beginning to the end of the novel.

Arun Joshi is not a solitary example of an author using the technique of fantasy in his novel to write a kind of political parable or satire. A contrast between the real and the unreal, the natural and the supernatural makes the satire effective.

There has been a growing 'trend towards fantasy in post-war writing.'[40] John Holloway goes on to explain :

> One can, of course, identify fantasy-writing earlier in the century. But its prominence and importance over the present period is new, and in an allegedly

great age of technological advance and materialist preoccupation this is a remarkable fact.[41]

NOTES AND REFERENCES

1. The Blurb to *The City and the River* (Orient Paperbacks, 1994).
2. *The City and the River,* p. 12.
3. *Ibid.*, p. 217.
4. *Ibid.*, p. 10.
5. *Ibid.*, p. 10.
6. *Ibid.*, p. 10.
7. *Ibid.*, p. 11.
8. *Ibid.*, p. 11.
9. *Ibid.*, p. 11.
10. *Ibid.*, p. 261.
11. *Ibid.*, p. 262.
12. *Ibid.*, p. 262.
13. *Ibid.*, p. 263.
14. *Ibid.*, p. 263.
15. *Ibid.*, p. 263.
16. *Ibid.*, p. 263.
17. *Ibid.*, p. 264.
18. *Ibid.*, p. 262.
19. Usha Bande, 'Archytypal Patterns in *The City and the River*' in R.K. Dhawan (ed.), *The Novels of Arun Joshi* (New Delhi, 1992), p. 259.
20. T.S. Eliot, *The Four Quartets* (London : Faber, n.d.) p. 23.
21. R.S. Pathak, 'Quest for Meaning in Arun Joshi's Novels' in R.K. Dhawan (ed.), *The Novels of Arun Joshi* (New Delhi, 1992), p. 64.
22. *Ibid.*
23. *The City and the River,* p. 10.
24. *Ibid.*, p. 262.
25. G.S. Amur, 'A New Parable', *Indian Literature,* No. 144, July-August 1991, p. 144.
26. E.M. Forster, *Aspects of the Novel* (Penguin Books, 1970), p. 115.
27. *Ibid.*, p. 115.
28. *Ibid.*, p. 117.
29. *Ibid.*, p. 117.
30. *Ibid.*, p. 121.

31. *Ibid.*, p. 121.
32. E.M. Forster, *Two Cheers for Democracy* (Penguin Books, 1974), p. 226.
33. E.M. Forster, *Aspects of the Novel* (Penguin Books, 1970), p. 118.
34. *The City and the River,* p. 42.
35. *Ibid.*, p. 44.
36. *Ibid.*, p. 133.
37. *Ibid.*, p. 133.
38. *Ibid.*, p. 134.
39. *Ibid.*, p. 217.
40. John Holloway, 'The Literary Scene' in *A New Pelican Guide to English Literature,* Vol. 8, *The Present,* (ed.), Boris Ford (Penguin Books, 1986), p. 99.
41. *Ibid.*, p. 99.

15

Seth's Use of Rhythm in *A Suitable Boy*

— Dr. Rama Kundu

INRODUCING an imaginary or real novelist and a novel within the novel has been a common practice with British fiction-writers since the 60s. Even earlier, Lawrence had toyed with the idea in *Mr. Noon* and Greene introduced Bendrix in *The End of an Affair*. Later Savedra and his novel were used in Graham Greene's *The Honorary Consul* and in *Monsignor Quixote* in order to lend perspective to the plights of Dr. Plarr and Father Quixote respectively as well as to bring into focus Greene's own preoccupations as a novelist. That an Indian writer in English of our times is as much English as Indian by his literary heritage is proved once again by Vikram Seth in his recent work. Vikram Seth's A *Suitable Boy* introduces an imaginary young writer, Amit Chatterjee, who like Mr. Seth, has already won fame and prizes for his poetical ventures abroad and is at the moment engaged, like Mr. Seth again, in writing a sprawling novel in the Indian context for the first time in his life. Amit describes the process of novel writing, or rather the kind of novel he writes, in terms of three images : the growth of a huge banyan tree, the exposition of an Indian classical *raag* and the flow of the Ganga. These observations of Amit appear to have a particular bearing on his author's novel as well. Indeed these three images, seen in perspective, seem to hold the key to certain basic structural features of the novel; at the same time these also pervade the texture and determine the mood, tenor and effect of various sequences in such a way as to remind the reader of Forster's use of 'rhythm' and 'pattern' in *A Passage to India.*

Like the typical modern writer Amit is mischievously evasive in face of potential or actual interviewers. However, he is frank with Lata — probably because of his special fondness for her — and confesses to her how regarding this first novel he is still unsure, in the process of finding out the adequate method or mode; while in the meantime, like a banyan tree, it sprouts, and grows, and spreads and drops down branches. Sometimes branches die. Sometimes the main trunk dies, and the structure is held up by the supporting trunks (483). Thus, once started, the growth of the work becomes, as it were, an elaborate and living process, it is rich, inclusive, varied and yet maintains a neat formal pattern.

In reference to Seth's own huge novel spread over nineteen books, the analogy seems to be no less befitting. Although the novel begins with one marriage and ends with another, contains lots of letters, domestic details, repeated allusions to Jane Austen, while maintaining a deceptively simple and apparently comic — ironic mode of story-telling, and thus may mislead the causal reader about the author's intentions, it is surely not that 'six inches piece of ivory' work. Depicted against the post-independence background of two years from 1950 to 1952. it narrates the saga of four families (the Kappors, the Mehras, the Chatterjees, and the Nawabs) with their members' private and public lives of joys and sorrows, it also inserts some real historical personages (including Jawaharlar Nehru) playing their respective roles in *real politick* inside and outside the parliament, and catches the pulsation of the throbbing life of millions of Indians during this transitional stage of Indian history. The wide variety of characters, the huge number of events in desperate and shifting settings, the continued pulsation of community life above and through disasters — riot, stampede, massacre, and the quiet rhythm of private lives interlaced with these public events in a remarkable variegated yet neat manner, should naturally recall that banyan tree analogy to the reader's mind. It is an intricate but living process, like that of the tree by which these, very many different elements have been made to coalesce with and merge into each other.

Even details of the peripheral elements become part of this organic, living process. As Amit would have put it...it has its own life — but so do the snakes and birds and bees and lizards and termites that live in and on it and off it...(483). It is in this way that the enormous variety and number of events, characters, settings, and other details have been accommodated in the novel with an air of perfect ease, while the spacious structure is comfortably held up by the 'main branches' or themes some of which, by the end of the novel, come to serve the role of supporting trunks. The events, big and small, offer a very wide spectrum in which the nineteen forty-seven separation in retrospect — the uprooted 'marginal man' fleeing across the borders, the debates and activities centering round the Zamindari Abolition Bill, the first general election in Independent India, a riot, a great Hindu mela followed by a greater disaster, the tremor of discontent and self-ssertion already being felt and voiced by the new generation in cities and remote villages, along with the innumerable events of so many private lives — have all been put in place. The characters range from monks and gurus, feudal lords, kings and Nawabs to the Prime-Minister, state ministers, and professional people from all walks of life including professors, writers, lowyets, doctors, musicians, courtesans, cobblers, formers, each of whom has his/ her respective place on this vast stage set by Seth. The setting too introduces a remarkable variety by means of a continuous shift across states and in-between sophisticated townships and remote village areas, small modern flats and old family mansions.

This assemblage of an enormous number of details helps the author to relate his story to a broader social context, and impart an epical dimension to what would otherwise have been but an extended story of a number of personal and familial relationship.

Amit also adds the analogy of the Ganga to that of the banyan tree to describe his novel. 'But then it's also like the Ganges in its upper, middle and lower course — including its delta' (483). The obvious thrust is on the linear course of narration which finally controls the 'sprouting branches of this 'banyan tree' spreading in so many different directions. Considered in this light, the 'delta' should be the ending of the novel, where the narrative, after gathering most of the loose threads, just as the river deposits its sediments at the delta, reaches its end. The narrative begins with Savita's marriage in 1950 and ends with Lata's marriage in 1952. Incidentally, the names of the four siblings — Arun, Varun, Savita, Lata — seem to echo a well — known Bengali folk-tale[2], also about siblings. 'Arun, Varun, Kiran, Mala (Mitra Majumdar 111-38) but in course of its linear progress the narrative embraces and unfolds so many more areas that finally the novel emerges as an enormous vista like the one that marks the progress of the Ganga from the upper through the middle to the lower course.

Again, Amit compares the exposition of an Indian classical *raag* to the process of novel-writing. In the big party at the Chatterjees, Amit comes to the rescue of Lata who had inadvertently spoken of the preference of Indian classical music to the utter dismay of Dr. Ila.

"I've always felt that the performance of a *raag* resembles a novel — or at least the kind of novel I'm attempting to write" (394). Amit continues, extemporizing as he goes along... "First you take one note and explore it for a while, then another to discover its possibilities, then perhaps you get to the dominant, and pause for a bit, and it's only gradually that the phrases begin to form and the tabla joins in with the beat...and then the more brilliant improvisations and diversions begin, with the main theme returning from time to time, and finally, it all speeds up and the excitement increases to a climax" (394). Here again one notes the same linear pattern from beginning through middle to end as suggested by the Ganga image; and also the elaboration, improvisations, diversions, the slow growth of a big text as indicated by the banyan tree image : What is further underscored by this musical allusion is a sense of sustained harmony-melody and rhythm-through a prolonged and highly elaborate process of narration. The uniqueness of the performance of an Indian classical *raag*, unlike the Western symphony, is that here the maestro is allowed a remarkable degree of freedom; provided he maintains a minimum frame of notations (called *Thaat*). Every singer is a free and original creator at every single performance of a ragg which could even take hours for complete exposition. Dr. lla, who has a book on metaphysical poetry, contemptuously dismisses Amit's fine *ex tempore* speech on the *raag*-novel relationship; "He's just a writer, he knows nothing about literature"(394). However, Seth's remarkable grasp of Indian classical music and his interesting ways of using it, especially in its aspect of creative fecundity and harmonious diversity are undeniably relevant in understanding this work..

I have heard learned professors of English dismissing *A Suitable Boy* as a frivolous book on old times written in conventional style. The book appears to have rather disappointed some admirers of *The Golden Gate*. The novel, however, could be considered from a different angle as well, both in regard to content and technique. To a perceptive reader, the novel may unfold itself as a tale vitally related and rhythmically referring to three clusters of images which thus serve as an integrating element bringing together the disparate and variegated material of the voluminous book under an organic unity : not the rigid unities of olden times but a subtler unity of content, mid, effect. The tree, the *raag*, and the Ganga are at the core of these three clusters respectively.

Let us consider the point in some details in respect of the first cluster. The banyan tree itself is mentioned twice besides Amit's use of it to explain his novelistic mode. Amit speaks of the big banyan tree in the Calcutta Botanical Garden by the Ganga. He invites Lata to picnic by the tree which is supposed to be very famous, the "biggest" in the world, as Tapan brags. Lata accepts the invitation gladly, but it is put off till Lata fails to avail herself of the promise of a romantic charming day under it. This tree repeatedly mentioned in course of their brief acquaintance — reflects on the quality of relationship between Lata and Amit. Lata is attracted by the soothing charm of the famous man; but she is also apprehensive that life with Amit may mean for her a loss of identity. This tree, as it is avidly described by Amit and Tapann, appears to have lost its original trunk while a crowd of supporting trunks hold it; this simultaneously attracts her and makes her feel uneasy. That Lata cannot and will not marry Amit is indicated by her hesitant response to the invitation. The image of the banyan tree appears ambiguous as to its implications in this context, it appears even more ambiguous when considered in the context of Saeeda Bai's observation; the courtesan mentions Mahesh Kapoor the minister as "a wood-cutter" to his son Maan; "it is very difficult to cut down a banyan tree, Daag Sahib, especially one that has been rooted so long in the soil of this province" (335). This has direct reference to the minister's sincere work regarding the Zamindari Abolition Bill. Here is a banyan tree which will not and should not endure. But because of the very fact that it has been there deeply entrenched since such a long time, its destruction will also involve those who lived on and off it, the snake as well as the bird, but I can hear your father's impatient axe on the last of its trunks, soon it will be torn from the earth, she knows it as every body else, but she raises a question which Maan fails to answer; "The snakes will be driven from its roots and termites burned with its rotten woos. But what will happen to the birds and monkeys who sat or chattered in its branches" (335). (Incidentally both Saeeda Bai and Tasneem, her daughter-passed off as sister, are associated with a caged parakeet.) It is paradoxical that the very same system which had exploited Saeeda Bai, who represents the worst victimization under feudal power — she had been raped by the Nawab of Baitar and sexually harrassed by the Raja of Marh — is yet so helplessly dependent on the very same people who pay her for the pleasure they extract, that she has no choice. Saeeda Bai's allusion to the banyan tree here serves as an excellent summing up of the situation in the early 50s on the eve of the introduction of the Zamindari Abolition Bill,-expectations and fears roused by the new era.

The changing times is one of the many themes of *A suitable Boy*. This change involves not only the feudal system but also an overall transition which has been set in train by the separation and independence. As justice Chatterjee sadly ponders : "who would have thought that things would have changed as much and as swiftly as they had" (468). He compares the Calcutta Gazettes of 1947 and 1948 and the smile disappears from his face : because "in microcosm these two pages reflected the passage of an empire and the birth of two countries from the idea tragic and ignorant that people of different religions could not peaceable live together in one" (469).Consequent to this tragic transition, Kedarnath and

Veena have been uprooted from their family mansion and propertied security of Lahore; they have come back to settle at the poorer quarters of Brahmpur. But they still grow a 'roofgarden;' the plants are small without roots into the earth, yet they are fresh and green. This is emblematic of the indomitable spirit and will of the couple who represent a new generation that will survive in spite if the scars and multilation of separation. The scars on Kedarnath's palms will remain as deep as the memory of "the cries of the blood — mad mobs on the streets of Lahore' (21) in his mother's consciousness. But Kedarnath would never show it off or even mention it; he would rather try to negotiate with his new situation, and his 'roof-garden derives its significance in the context of this heroic, dignified struggle.'

The legend that operates behind the 'pul mela' is, again, related to the leaves of a mythical 'pippal' tree which botanically belongs to the same family as the banyan tree. The myth has survived through centuries just like these ageless trees which have amazing power for continuance, and thus may serve as a counterpoint to the suggestions of changing times. Other big trees recur in various scenes in such a way that one such scene would automatically call back to another and thus would help the reader to 'connect', to perceive the subtle inter — connection among apparently disconnected elements, including people, scenes, moods, sequences. The tall gulmohurs in bloom is accociated in Lata's mind with her father's death ("It was in April that he died. Gulmohurs were then in bloom too—") (137), and paradoxically with her own love, its early joy and later pain. Again the dark orange flowers lay thick below her feet (1332) as they did last year and also years ago. In the early days of their shy friendship Lata and Kabir would casually meet by some big tree, with a huge solid knotty trunk. The freguent and rhythmic references to various trees in this novel-some very big, some smaller which continue to strike roots into the earth and spring blossoms towards the sky while lovers separate, people pass away under them — seem to lend an assurance of something solid, sustaining, mysterious, evergrowing, everbecoming. The message they give is that the individual's trauma or ecstasy in not the be-all and end-all, that there is still something which had been prior to and will remain beyond it. A person of rare intuitive goodness could have a mystic communion with this transcendental life. The self-effacing Mrs. Mahesh Kapoor, whose first name gets lost behind her role as wife and mother, the outwardly unimpressive woman who yet commands an extraordinary goodness, has an instinctive affinity with trees big and small. Trees, as it were, respond to her affection by doing their best. Thus, the gulmohur in her garden has petals "almost-scarlet, rather than the usual red —orange." Looking at the bloom Savita lovingly thinks : "Everything appeared more intense in the garden at Prem Nivas. It was almost as if the plants understood that their mistress, though she would not avertly complain about a weak performance, would not be happy with less than the best," (175). Mrs. Kapoor has been, however, known to suffer chronically from a seasonal allergy caused by the pollen of 'neem' flowers, yet she would not have the huge tree cut down; and when the labourers cut off some of its branches carelessly she is shocked and unhappy. Mrs. Kapoor achieves an intuitive communication with trees, plants, flowers, and this partly explains the mystery of the unaccountable charm of this lady who is apparently subdued, snubbed, hectored by a domineering husband, with her embracing love for people, disinterested affection for husband and children, her love for the house, and especially with her delight in the garden she reminds one a little of Ruth Wilcox of *Howard's End.* As long after that old woman's death Margaret comes to the conviction of feeling that "she is everything. She is the house, and the tree that leans over it" (292). In a similar way Mrs. Kapoor's garden too, along with the harsingar tree she loves so, seems to be an extension of her own self. Seth's description of tree unmistakably suggests the link between the two. A modest unhandsome tree by day, the harsingar becomes "glorious" at nights, "full of a delicate fragrance but the tiny flowers with their hearts come wafting down at dawn." And tonight it would again be full. And the flowers would again float down as the sun rose. Then follows the comment: The tree flowered, but kept noting for itself (1042). It is significant that for Mrs. Kapoor who loves all the trees. "There is no tree like it at all" (1042).

She even plans to plant a seedling at the backgarden of

Pran's house, so that it will always be as old as Uma, Pran's baby-daughter. Like the harsingar, Mrs. Kapoor has given away her love, her energy, her years without reserve or complain, and now through this tree she will continue to be at the side of her grand-daughter as a fragrant soothing presence. Again, the tree which gives away all its flowers at dawn only to be luxuriously refilled every night thus repeats the continuous cycle of birth-death-rebirth, a concept central to the Hindu-belief to which Mrs. Kapoor fondly clings. It is notable that like Ruth Wilcox, she too is a frail woman already in the process of the fading out as the story takes off and whereas her overruling husband would rather avoid thinking of this possibility. She foresees the eventuality of death calmly and with even eager fortitude since the end is, to her Indian mind, but part of that cyclic process of birth, death and rebirth which she must complete before attaining to the final release, "of course I am determined to die." Mrs. Kapoor says, "How else can I go through my rebirths and finally end them" (1026). The story of an individual life seen thus, appears to become part of an elaborate process which is repeated by the trees. Old trunks die while new branches sprout up to become supporting trunks, the unending cycle of blossom-fall-blossom rotates on, the flow of the Ganga — eternal yet never the same wave, also reiterates a similar process. Mrs. Kapoor and the harsingar become one and the same as both submit gracefully to this process of life. It may be mentioned that Maan seeks the Harsingar flower twice after his mother's death. He fails to have one, because once the season is over, and the other time the place where he looks for it is not his mother'garden. However, his very remembrance of the flower on those two occasions is significant. The first time he yearns for it also marks his first coming to terms with his prison life, his anguish and bereavement. It is as it were, his mother's inherent peace is being restored to him as he remembers the flowers in this mood of sad resignation, "Once he asked for a few harsingar flowers from the garden of Prem. Nivas and Veena had told him that the season was over" (1230). Again, on the evening of Lata's marriage "for a moment he (Maan) wondered where the harsingar tree was, before he realized that he was in a different garden altogether" (1340). This calls back to the other marriage at the opening of the novel : "The newly-weds were escorted to a flower shrouded bench near a sweet-smelling, rough-leafed harsingar tree in white-and-orange bloom" (17). And wishes and greetings fell on the couple as copiously as those delicate flowers fall to the ground at dawn (17). And Mrs. Kapoor feels very happy for the sudden, prolific blossoming of the harsingar tree" at this time, which she believes to be a sign of "the grace of gods whose prized and contested possession, in mythical times, it used to be" (17). So many ups and downs have taken place between these two marriages, the world has changed for Maan. Yet at this moment he will attain to the peace of complete reconcilement with Firoz who had been so dear till they were so suddenly estranged on that fatal evening at Saeeda Bai's. As Maan, standing alone, sad, nostalgic. looks for the harsingar tree "Firoz came up to him,, and they stood there, silent." An eloquent silence of love, peace, fulfilment. Thus the rhythmic recurrence of a tree serves to connect the beginning with the end, while subtly uniting a number of moments, ideas and characters lying scattered through the book.

Flowers also form part of this cluster of tree/plant imagery. As Maan and Firoz stand together after a long time, — in silent happiness — "a rose petal or two floated down from somewhere. Neither bothered to brush it off." This again calls back to an earlier occasion, *i.e.,* Pran's marriage, when rose-petals "float (ed) down form nowhere" to stick to Mann's cap, and Firoz gently brushed it away (20). Since then they have been through ordeals of passion and remorse so that now they can accept life with poise. Flowers coming down silently over scenes of individual sorrows and joys — equally transient and yet fragrant and beautiful, each in its own way — lend a broader perspective as well as an aesthetic flavour to the respective contexts. Again, after her brilliant night-long musical performance at Prem Nivas on the occasion of *Holi* Saeeda Bai suddenly feels weary and gets up to take a stroll through the garden. This is a rare moment for her, when sad peaceful alone, she touches the glossy leaves of a pomelo tree." And though harsingar is "no longer in bloom" : a jacaranda flower dropped down (like this one night of exquisite) music and joy which passed away so quickly) in the darkness. She looked up and smiled to herself a little sadly (88). Lata parts from Kabir, tousles the leaves gently, and "a shower of fragrant petals fell on her hair" (186). The brief, diurnal life — span of these delicate exquisite flowers helps to bring out the quality of their youthful, fresh charming yet brief romance. Again, there will be another flock of flowers on the very same branches next morning — the expression of the unaffected, abundant energy of life which survives through all events, — mundane or catastrophic.

Mrs. Rupa Mehra is inordinately fond of roses, Saeeda Bai too has a preference for roses, but her expression is less clamorous and more artistic. She has a small rose-coloured house and whenever Maan enters her place, he is greeted by the scent of rose-*attar*. Mrs. Mehra is the proud matriarch having all young people calling her "Ma" whereas the latter has to suppress the mother within her and is compelled by society to play the role model of a paramount instead. However, their common association with the same flower helps the reader to see the subtler connection.

Tending flowers makes an important item in Mrs. Kapoor's daily itinerary. Once Pran asks his ailing mother why doesn't she call the *mali* into the house where it is cool, and give him his instructions there. She protests vehemently : "Oh no — That wouldn't work at all. It could have a bad effect on the morale of the flowers." With her disinterested goodness, and her readiness to accept and get merged into the blossomfall — blossom cycle epitomized by the floral world, and held as an inherent truth of life by the Hindu mystic. Mrs. Kapoor automatically achieves an instinctive communication with flowers; it is in growing plants and making them blossom that she finds a kind of self expression, and attains to a sort of fulfilment. On the eve of death, Mrs. Kapoor is seen, significantly, in association with her flowers. Pran, after visiting Mann in Jail, comes to Prem Nivas to find his mother lying on a sofa on the verandah. She has looked forward to all these days as fulfilment. She was facing the garden which was full of early flowers : pansies, calendulas, gerberas, salvias, cosmos, phlox and a few California poppies. Even insects and birds seem to be in tune with this scene of joyous fulfilment which is to last only through one night; "Bees were buzzing around the first few lemon-scented blossoms on the pomelo tree, and a small glossy blue-bleak sunbird flitted in and out of its branches" (1216). Pran, fatigued under the mounting pressure of worries including his brother's trial, his mother's failing health, his own chronic sickness, has at this moment a sudden flash of realization. He sees that in spite of so many problems and disasters two things at least continued to survive and sustain through everything : "His mother's sustaining goodness, and the continuing peace of the garden" (1216). The two reflect on each other, and together create the soothing effect of "peace" that ultimately covers the scars of all "wars", or evoke the flow of the Ganga that would rise again and again to wash away all stains of violence, sorrow, catastrophe. Lata's marriage thus provides the appropriate terminating point of the narration, and though it takes place on a hot day, " the trees," the author takes care to mention "champa, jacaranda, and Sita ashok — (all big tress) were full of white or mauve or red blossom, and bougainvillaea (a creeper)-orange, red, pink and magenta-fell in great masses over the walls of the house and down the trunks of tress." A scene of luxuriant bloom : once again. Incidentally, the name of Lata, who provides a sort of narrative centre to the novel, means a creeper which has to cling to a tree for sustenance and blossoming.

In *Howards End,* E.M. Forster made an interesting use of Beethoven's fifth symphony. The three-parts symphony with its risefall, rise-rhythm has been made central to the structure of the novel, the image-pattern, the symbolism, the pattern of moods. In *A Suitable Boy* the exposition of an Indian classical *raag* serves a similar purpose. Amit explains to Dr. Ila how the *raag* is slowly performed step by step through elaboration, diversification, rich ecstasy, climax and conclusion while the main melody or tune continues to be at the core as the controlling central tune. This, according to him, throws light also on the way his novel is made. In the novel this performance has been described repeatedly. It is in this context that the character of Ustad Majeed Khan attains significance. This music maestro., who otherwise plays no role in furthering the realistic action, is still remembered by the reader as he, again and again is seen at performing some particular *raag*. As he starts singing a *raag* it casts a spell on the listener who, for the time being forgets personal troubles and involvements. Thus, Lata, Kabir, Malati and others listen to him performing in the hall, Ishaaq khan listens to his morning *raag* over the A.I.R. and later face to face at the Ustad's House. As a person the Ustad could be rude, mean, uninteresting. But when he sings he attains to a different identity. At those moments he is a mystic visionary, in whose mind different religions get merged, their border lines get effaced in one moment of rare vision. Music is his livinghood, his joy and his religion too, a religion made of divine vibrations : "Music too was prayer to him, and some mornings he would be up long before dawn to sing 'Lolit' or some other early *raag*. Then the first words of the azaan ringing about God's greatness 'would vibrate across the rooftops in the cool air." When he heard the words calling people from their sleep "he would smile. It was one of the pleasures of his day" (296). The Ustad is worried that if the proposed Shiva temple is built by the mosque's side, there should be disharmony, the music of this early call might clash with the conch; it is in this disturbed state of mind that the Ustad begins meditatively to hum the words of the composition — 'Jaago Mohan Pyaare' (A familiar tune to the lovers of Hindustani music) "Humming it, he forgot himself. He forgot the room he was in and the students still waiting for their lessons. It was very far from his mind that the words were addressed to the dark god Krishna, asking him to wake up with the arrival of morning or that 'Bhairava' — the name of the raag he was singing — was an epithet of the great Shiva himself" (296). Here the Ustad has his moment of epiphary through music when all disharmonies get dissolved into one all-embracing ecstasy of melody. And this music in its turn gets merged into the other image — that of the Ganga, the eternal flow, all-embracing, all dissolving.

There are also abundant references to other forms of music which are comparatively brief, but stirring, touching and harmonious in their own ways nevertheless. Thus, Saeeda Bai sings here excellent *Ghazals, i.e.*, lighter classical music based on *raag*. The speciality of a Ghazal is that through its various diversifications and improvisations, it will fall back again and again on some particular refrain of a melody. Thus, in a *Ghazal* we have a miniature form of what happens in the total book — something like an elaborate exposition of some Indian classical *raag* which, again, is like the narrative process in which some main themes recur through a wide range of diversifications. There are also references to *Rabindra-sangeet* (Tagore's songs). Amit's mother, representing the older generation, is still fascinated by Tagore's songs and works, though to her children he is R.N. Tagore, what a bore!" Readers familiar with Rabindra-sangeet know that these songs are often based on a classical raag as it is presented in its barest outlines. The most familiar form of Tagore's song follows the four-part *Dhrupadi* form : *sthayee* (1st part), *antara* (2nd part), *sanchari* (3rd part), *abhog* (4th part) : this is like a complete performance of a classical *raag* being compressed into a nutshell. Meenakshi and kuku who represent the post-independence new class apparently out of tune with old India, also characteristically fail too be drawn either towards the Tagorean melody or the classical music. In spite of their piano-thumping and limerick — improvisations they fail to be part of the rich harmonious life of India as represented by the Ustad's 'Bhairav.' At the end Dr. Kishan Seth would rather have Saeeda Bai singing on the occasion of Lata's marriage. But in view of recent memories the plan is given up and Saeeda Bai is replaced by the *Sanai* players. Thus, at the end, it is once again return from the microcosm of *ghazal* to the macrocosm of fullfledged exposition of a classical *raag* which is like the banyan in its elaboration and rich diversity and like the Ganga in it linear progress from the beginning through the middle to the end. Ganga is alluded to as recurring point of reference. Savita is married off early in the novel; she settles down happily in her new life. In the meantime "the broad silty-brown Ganga continues flowing due East" (32), reflecting on the quality of fullness and peace of the new couple's life. Some time later Pran has troubles in his place of work due to the power-mongering of influential people. But Pran can take it in his stride as a matter of course, and as he recalls Tagore's lines of admonition against meanness, he has an epiphany, a vision of the entire length of the Ganga from the Prayag to the delta. "He (Pran) followed it first downstream to Patna and Calcutta, an upstream past Benaras till it divided at Allahabad" (54). This vision not only soothes Pran; it also makes room for a broader perspective in which these mean intrigues get reduced to the trifles they are.

Again, Lata and Kabir during their stealthy trip to Barsaat Mahal on the eve of the confession of mutual love which they could resist, take a boatride on the quiet river. The Barsaat Mahal, a centre of various activities, is now "transfigured into something of abstract and fine beauty. Above its sheer river-wall it rose, its reflection in the water almost perfect, almost unrippled." The river seems to have come to a standstill. But one knows it is but an illusion, a kind of romantic dream. Does it reflect on their love, which is going to be another transient dream, sort of painting in water, bound to be shattered by the slightest breeze, and never to be realised in life. But the Ganga will continue its flow. She treasures the memory of past shadows in her bosom but that will not deter her flow.

The Ganga is there, continuing presence. at the back of human scenes, their relationships, joys and fears. Mrs. Kapoor, along with her son, daughter, daughter's husband and his mother, had a long wait before they could secure an appointment with Ramjap Baba on the eve of the mela.' Facing the Ganga, the Baba is chanting absent-mindedly "Thank you, thank you" and the team slowly go ahead, "she (Mrs. Kapoor) her son, his sister, her husband, and his mother — a chain of love and, consequently of fear — moved slowly out or the crush on to the open" (726). The intense but frail individual life is placed in perspective as the monk with his face towards the Ganga chants "Thank you, thank you." It is a continuous thanks giving that relates him to the other monk by the river — Sanaki baba, who teaches Dipankar "to accept" (748) life with resignation. In this act of unquestioning acceptance, the two monks get identified with the all — embracing flow of the Ganga which accepts flowers and corpses with equal indifference and benediction, After the disastrous stampede at the 'Pul Mela' signs of the event remain traceable for a while reminding people of the memories of looses, anguish and terror, But ultimately the Ganga covers up all. "In time the Ganga rose with the monsoon rains and covered the sands," Only Ramjap Baba remains on his platform, "surrounded now on all sides by the Ganga, and continued to recite unceasingly the eternal name of God" (752).

If two main 'branches' of the 'banyan tree' are to be identified those should be the two themes centering round the issues of love and marriage and friendship, the first focusing on Lata, and the second on Maan and Firoz. Lata, inspite of her painful love for Kabir slowly realises that she couldn't give up her family. When both Pran and Savita are hospitalized she realizes it more clearly, 'with life and death so near each other here in the hospital, it seems to Lata that all that had provided continuity in the world or protection from it was the family (877). This realization helps her to make up her mind finally regarding Kabir. This experience of coming to terms with life gets artistic expression through the image of back water. Lata talks to Savita's baby (who is of course incapable of responding). "what if we are quite happy to paddle our canoe in a pleasant little backwater — and are not interested in the Niagra falls and the Barsaat Mahal" (879). The backwater, however, is not entirely unaffected by the mainstream.. but repeats, although in a very subdued way, the rising tide and falling ebb of the river out there just as the tune in a lower key could repeat the main tune played on a higher key, or a smaller branch of a big tree could repeat the same pattern as displayed by a bigger branch. It is a series of such rhythmic repetitions that Seth introduces to place his tale of individual lives in a broad social context and a broader time-space continuum. And this tale has been placed in per-spective again and again by being continually referred to the image of the Ganga. As Pran and Savita return from Barssai Mahal by boat at night — Pran has in the meantime recovered from his illness though the shadow of death haunts still-they have inhaled the peace of the Ganga which emanates from its eternal flow onwards.

"Quietly they moved down the clam and sacred river that had come down to earth so that its waters might flow over the ashes of those long dead, and that would continue to flow long after the human race had, through hatred and knowledge burned it self out" (1070). The Ganga is not just another river to the Indian imagination. It is an archetypal image. From ancient hymns to folklores, from epics and legends to modern texts it has remained a powerfully evocative image for the Indian reader, even more than banyan tree or the *raag* 'Bhairav' which are also characteristically Indian in the very special appeal and significance they carry for the average Indian reader. Thus, the three images together, as they operate rhythmically, impart a very special flavour to the novel, which one might define as "Indianness." It is not the 'Indianness' which so provokes Brunton aganist Raja Rao, *i.e.,* "eccentricity and freakishness" (212-222). Brunton however concedes to another form on Indianness. His claim is that Indian society, unlike the western, is still a group society, and thus "even individual dramas tend to have a broad social context and one life reflects another." And the novelist can thus draw upon certain situations, essentially individual, which yet have almost the archetypal power of parable. (215). Seth has precisely done that, and done it quite artistically.

Seth, as an Indian writer of our times. has naturally drifted far from the nationalistic ego of the early Indian writers in English, as well as from the later phase of guilt-conscious, painfully self-conscious writers represented by Anand, Raja Rao, or even the anguished bewilderment of *Azadi* or *A Train* to *Pakistan*, that accompanied the trauma of 1947. Seth has absorbed the difficulties and shocks sustained by the preceding generations of Indian writers in English and has given back something wonderful. It is positive, poised, courageous approach, which is not an usual thing to come across either in the expatriates or in the resident Indian novelists. This poise lends him a power of self-distancing and thus enables him to sustain a genial rarely bitter, never caustic, placidity of narrative style. Seth had been famous with *The Golden Gate*. But with *A Suitable Boy* he reaches maturity, both as a visionary and as an artist. To say the least, with this book, Seth has stirred "Great Expectations, in the common Indian reader."

REFERENCES

1. "In *The Honorary Consul* Saavedra's fictions...form an integral part of the narrative. Savedra's darkly romantic themes...are set before us in the first pages of the book and their presence is felt like an undersong during the events and emotions unfolding themselves in the rest of the story.

   Green's use of his own and Saavedra's fiction to comment obliquely on each other this manner is an allusion to current narrative devices (such as those of John Fowles) Miriam Allott, "Surviving the Course, or a Novelist for all Seasons, Graham Green's *The Honorary Consul," The Uses of Fiction*, D. Jefferson and G. Martin (ed.), The Open University Press, Stratford, England,. 1982, pp. 237-148.

2. The writer of *A Suitable Boy* appears to be particularly conversant in Bengali culture, the novel gives enough hints of his familiarity with the language too, including Bengaliphrase-idioms. Is it possible that he has picked up this well-knowh Bengali tale to borrow a nomenclature which would immediately send a ring of recognition to his Bengali readers. Again, the folktale also underscores the theme of strong family ties, especially among siblings and their mother.

WORK CITED

Brunton, T.D. Indian in Transition : The Heritage of Indianness, *Critical Essays on Indian Writing in English*, Naik-Desai Amur (ed.), Macmillan, Indian 1977.

Forster, E. M. Howard's End. 1910 Penguin International 1870, Mitra Majumdar, D.R. *Thakumar Jhuli* : *Banglar Rupkatha* (Grandma Bag : Folktales of Bengal), 1907 Mitra Ghosh Calcurra, 1983.

Seth Vikram : *A Suitable Boy*, Viking, Indian Penguin Books, 1983.

16

A Broad Study on *The God of Small Things*

—*Dr. John E. Abraham*

A cross-stitch pattern, a criss-cross of contrasts in emotions, language and movement of time, *The God of Small Things* is superb in its architectonics. Violent love and violent hate from the warp and woof. The omniscient narrator chooses the time of Rahel's home coming on Estha's re-return to start the story. But the narrator is not impartial. She takes sides with Rahel, who seems to be her prime concern. Rahel is shown at two points of time : at the age of seven, and at the age of thirtyone, the latter being "a viable die-able age" (p. 3) at which Ammu, Rahel's mother, died. The two major emotions of the narrator are love for Ammu and hatred for Baby Kochamma. This theme of love and hate is built up by innumerable loops of contrasts or opposites in language and movement of time.

Most often the narrator seems to identify with Rahel resulting in the false impression that Rahel is the narrator. The reference to the characters as Baby Kochamma (Navomi Ipe), Margaret Kochamma, Mamachi (Soshamma) and Pappachi (Benaan John Ipe) helps creating the wrong impression. The narrator's hatred of Baby Kochamma is so great that every act of hers, every word of her and even her pet name Baby is laughed at. Chacko introduces her to his ex-wife and child "My aunt, Baby" and Sophie Mol's response in the words of the narrator : "But aunt babies confounded her." (p. 144). The narrator does not take into account the generation gap between Baby and Ammu. Baby, brought up under the Victorian idea of morality, does not seem to be obsessed with the women's need as Ammu is. She graciously accepts the man-less-woman-state, while Ammu quarrels with it. Her love for the Irish priest Father Mulligan is a foil to Ammu's love for Velutha.

> She pictured them together, in dark sepulchral rooms with heavy velvet drapes, discussing Theology. That was all she wanted. All she ever dared to hope for. Just to be near him. Close enough to smell his beard. To see the coarse weave of his cassock. To love him just by looking at him (p. 24).

But the narrator does not stress the point that Baby is also a rebel, a progressive by the standards of her day. She became a Roman Catholic and tried to become a nun. But, when she discovered that it was of no use, she made her parent take her back home. She remains in love with Father Mulligan, who also returns her love in his own fashion. They keep up a correspondence till the death of the Irish priest who became a Hindu Sanyasi in the evening of his life. Even after his death, Baby continues the ritual of writing in her diary "I love you. I love you" (p. 298).

This is ridiculous in the narrator's opinion. She seems to believe that 'living' as far as a woman is concerned is having orgasm. "She danced for him. On the boat-shaped piece of earth she lived" (p. 337). "The Cost of Living" is a glorious epilogue to feminism and free sex that Ammu craves for. It describes sex in its full glory, and the last word "Tomorrow" is suggestive of the ever-lasting dominance, supremacy of carnal passion over human intelligence. Thus, the novel is a justification of Ammu's woman's needs as well as an atonement for the death of the innocent 'god of small things,' Velutha.

Sophie Mol's death is only a marker of the movement of time as well as action — "After Sophie Mol's Funeral" (p. 11), "That was only days before she died" (p. 135). Chacko breaks the door of Ammu's room and order her to get out of the house because of his daughter's death. It is her death that necessitates the 'Return' of Estha. But the narrator very deftly uses the event as an icing to hide the cake under.

The real action of the novel takes place within a fortnight, between Sophie Mol's arrival and her funeral. The duration of the sex-episode lasts fourteen nights. And twentythree years later, the action is reviewed through the perspective of the favourite character, Rahel. Naturally, the bias and prejudice of Rahel find a place in the narrative. Rahel's distrust of Baby Kochamma and Baby Kochamma's distrust of Rahel are movement and counter movement of a psychic symphony.

In medieval terminology, Baby Kochamma is the villain, Ammu, the tragic heroine and Velutha, the brave knight-errant. Baby Kochamma is said to plot the scheme from the very beginning. She tries to transform the two-egg twins, Rahel and Estha, into cultural ambassadors of India to their British cousin who is two years older to them. Her efforts fall flat on two accounts. One, the two-egg twins refuse to rise up to the mark. Two, their English cousin is a better strategist than they. Sophie Mol wants Rahel to leave one ant alive. "Let's leave one alive so that it can be lonely," (p. 186). She gives the twins "an involved, though somewhat inaccurate description of sex" (p. 135). Rahel's calling her "Thimble-drinker" (p. 135) seems to be scatology.

Velutha, the innocent victim of callous society, is more cultured than the Brahmin-convered-Syrian Christians and the touchable Nairs. When the children dress themselves in saris and present themselves at his hut as Mrs. Pillai, Mrs. Eapen and Mrs. Rajagopalan, Velutha keeps up the fiction and joins them in the play. He introduces them to his paralysed brother and gives them tender coconuts to drink. He chats with them as if they are adults and gives them each a wooden spoon by way of present. He loves the children and plays with them as per their requirements. The children love him by day and their mother loves him by night, and the love brings to him savage brutal death. He is certainly "the God of Loss."

The board outline of the narrative technique is that of Kathakali, which Rahel has learned to love and appreciate under K.N.M. Pillai's guidance. In Kathakali, the story is known to everybody, yet the artist captures the viewer's imagination by the way of its presentation. Arundhati Roy remarked on a BBC interview that her training in architecture tremendously helped her in writing the novel. She follows architectural methodology. The introductory chapter is an index to the reader regarding the main events and characters. But the way "the bleached bones" (p. 33) of the story are stuffed and restored to shape evinces a master's skill.

The common ingredients of epic narrative are used with great effect. Even minor characters are described in detail *e.g.*, the description of Latha, Comrade Pillai's niece who never appears again (p. 270-271). Inversions and repetitions are used in plenty for the sake of emphasis. "But Rahel Comrade Pillai knew well" (p. 14). Estha in "beige and pointy shoes" is repeated many times (p. 94, 115, 145, 193, 196, 226...). Often the repetitions are insignia. "Fountain in Love in-Tokyo" is Rahel, "A brown leaf on his black back" is Valutha (p. 73). Estha walks past the pots and pans through the Paradise Pickle Factory; "Past glass casks of vinegar with corks/Past shelves of pectin and preservatives. Past trays of bitter gourd,..." (p. 193). The march of policemen through the compound of the `History House' is another example : "Past ancient trees cloaked in vines....Past a deep blue beetle...Past gaint spider webs...." (p. 305). The three words "seaked, Healed, Untapped" have a Miltonic ring.

The post-modern morality of the novel is pure biology (masturbation, free sex, incest). The private parts of the human body have a fascination for Rahel, the favourite of the narrator. She is dismissed from a convent school because she has bumped against senior girls to find out whether breasts hurt. On the way to Cochin, at the level-crossing, Rahel sees the lunatic Muralidharan sitting on the milestone. "His balls and penis dangled down" (p. 62). At the air-port the baby who "thought he was the Pope" smiled and waved at the people around him, "with his penis in a bottle" (p. 139). K.N.M. Pillai's nipple peeped at Rahel over the top of the boundary wall (p. 129). Baby Kochamma's breasts are "melons" (p. 98). Estha's bottom is "Tight plums in drain pipes" (p. 104)... The list is not exhausted.

But the narrator draws up the children, Estha and Rahel at seven, with real insight into child psychology. They know that Ammu loves them double for she is both their father and mother. Estha's concern for Ammu is seen when he buys the ticket to Ayemenem on the return trip from the police station. Rahel denies herself the hotel dinner, a self-inflicted punishment for having hurt Ammu. She is tormented by the feeling that Ammu has begun to love her less. The children try to find in Chacko a father-surrogate, but Chacko is ignorant of their need. They are intelligent, energetic and mischievous. They play Shakespeare "Ettu Kochu Maria." They read backwards. They tell Miss Mitten that 'Malayalam' and 'Madam I'm Adam' are the same when read backwards and forwards (Palindrome). Miss. Mitten tells Baby Kochamma that she has seen Satan in their eyes. Months later Miss. Mitten is run down by a milk van in reverse gear. To the twins there was "hidden justice in the fact that the milk van had been reversing" (p. 60).

Some of Rahel's ideas are fantastic. The twins row the boat repaired by Velutha, on the floor of his hut. On the wall there is a calendar with the picture of Jusus : "calendar-Jesus with lipstick and rouge, and lurid, jewelled heart glowing through his clothes" (p. 208). The seven year old Rahel thinks : "He walked on water. Perhaps. But could He have *swum* on land?" (p. 211). Similarly her question to Chacko : "Is it necessary that people have to love their own children most in the World?" (p. 118) makes us examine closely the socially accepted love laws.

Roy has produced some unforgettable characters. One among them is the Orangedrink Lemondrink man behind the Refreshments Counter in the Abhilash Talkies, who waits like a spider with the web spread to catch energetic young boys who chance to come with a tune of *The Sound of Music* on their lips. Another one is the willy comrade K.N.M. Pillai, built in the mould of a Casca or Cassius, exhibiting a 'hungry look' and for whom harted, jealousy and ambition are the motivating impetuses. Baby Kochamma who keeps her self isolated in "the old house on the hill" is like Miss Havisham in the *Great Expectations.*

The narrator's sense of language and humour can never be adequately praised. Baby Kochama's "staged charity" of "forcebathing" a village child (p. 23), Estha's first "adult assignment" to urinate alone in the toilet (p. 97), the yellow teeth of the Orangedrink Lemondrink man : "They saw, they smiled, they sang, they smelled, they moved, They mesmerized" (p. 102) are a few examples. The Orangedrink Lemondrink man wiped his marble counter and waited — "And waiting he wiped, and wiping he waited" (p. 101) reminds us of Shelley's skylark "singing and soaring and soaring and singing." The play on the Latin phrase 'Locus standi'; on later, "Lay Ter;" the combinations of opposites like "bottomless-bottomful feelings" (p. 107); inventions like "greenmossing" (p. 10) "getting-outedness" (p. 172) "Sad-About-Joe silence" (p. 173), "Stoppited" (p. 141) "Men's Needs entrance" (p. 295), and the use of Malayalam words in English spelling, illustrate the narrator's bold use of language. Most often the similes exhibit a keen sense of humour. One example will do. Lenin, K.N.M. Pillai's son, dressed in yellow shirt and black shorts is compared to a taxi, "dressed like a taxi" (p. 132).

They are many stylistic similarities between Roy and Salman Rushdie. A few of them are given below :

1. The use of Indian words with English spellings :

   e.g., "Mundus", Raksha"; "Ed Cherukka", : "Chacko Saar Vannu"

   (p. 52, 59, 101, 171, *The God of Small Things*).

   "Vilayat"; "djinni"; "Pagal Khanna"

   (p. 4, 48, 346, *The Satanic Verses*).

2. Making compound words by using hyphens :

   "Mitten-shaped", "Ammu-eyes", "trying-not-to-cry mouth"

   (p. 82, 96, 300, *The God of Small Things*).

   "my mother says your're-the-fairy-queen"; "red-and -white-stripped", "high-risk"

   (p. 332, 428, 435, *The Satanic Verses*).

3. Spell out letters of a word for special effect

   "Dee Ay Em En" (damn)

   (p. 182, *The God of Small Things*).

   "Ellowen Decowen" (London)

   (p. 42, *The Satanic Verses*).

4. Use of italics for a part of a sentence or a full sentence :

"Why *should she?, I'm sorry, Colonel Sabhapathy, but I'm afraid I've said my say,*"

(p. 21, 63, *The God of Small Things*).

"But *where* have you been,"

(p. 36, *Midnight's Children*).

"*-And I'm back*"

(p. 353, *The Satanic Verses*).

5. Using phrases on their own *i.e.*, a phrase in parenthesis as a full sentence :

"a viable die-able age". "A rushing, rolling, fish swimming sense".

(p. 3, 30, *The God of Small Things*).

"The watery Caliban", "The doomed Hummingbird"

(p. 10, 39, *Midnght's Children*).

6. Use of topical references

"Adoor Basi", "Comrade E.M.S. Namboodiripad"

(*The God of Small Things*).

"Sreedevi" *(The Satanic Verses*).

"J.P. Narayan and Morarji Desai"

(p. 499, *Midnight's Children*).

7. Frequent references to famous writers, books and its characters :

"Sydney Carton", "The Tempest abridged by Charles and Mary Lamb"

(p. 61, 59, *The God of Small Things*).

"Caliban", "Quran"

(p. 10, 4, *Midnight's Children*).

"the English critic Kenneth Tyanan had imagined the polysyllabic characters in Marlowe's Tamburlaine the great...."

(p. 525, *The Satanic Verses*).

8. Writing words together as if they are a single word :
"Yesyesyesyesyes", "thiswayandthat"

(p. 56, 107, *The God of Small Things*).

"getoutofitsillyoldmoo, itsthesoddingbeach"

(p. 134, *The Satanic Verses*).

Even some narrative episodes in *The God of Small Things* and *The Satanic Verses* are alike. The twins in *The God of Small Things* and Salahuddin Chamchawala in *The Satanic Verses* have their existence rooted in the actual geographies of living and working spaces and such physical transmutations correspond with streams of private experiences. Rahel, Estha and Salahuddin try to make a home away from home. Salahuddin hates Bombay and goes to England and comes back to Bombay to look after his father. The twins after living in alien sphere return to Ayemenem. The 'homosexual experience of Estha at the hands of the Orangedrink Lemondrinkman' is similar to the one Salahuddin has :

> "In a hollow of black stone Salahuddin saw a man in dhoti bending over a pool. Their eyes met and man beckoned him with a single finger which he then laid across his lips. *Shh,* and the mystery of rock-pools drew the boy towards the stranger. He was a creature of bone spectacles framed in what might have been ivory. His fingers curling, curling, like a baited hook, come. When Salahuddin came down the other grasped him, put a hand around his mouth and forced his young hand between old and fleshless legs, to feel the freshbone there..." (p. *The Satanic Verses*).

Is it purely accidental that Ammu dies at thirtyone, Rahel narrates the story at thirtyone and Rushdie's narrator in *Midnght's Children,* Saleem Sinai, is at thirtyone. Also there is one passage in *Midnight's Children,* "Ask how many times the leather thongs wound round the handles of the litter — the answer in thirty-one" (p. 12).

Wide variety of images pertaining to different senses are used by Roy. The visual language they produce, is surprisingly sophisticated. Suggestive rather than explicit, they convey meaning in formulaic shorthand. They sometimes contradict and oppose each other. The contradictions and paradoxes alleviate the misery and aggrandize the mystery (*e.g.*, "The Pessimist and the Optimist" p. 238). The usual pattern of making the implicit the explicit is reverted here to achieve amazing results. Roy does not try to move from the abstract to the concrete, and from the far-off to the near and from the general to the particular. Instead, she carries the reader from the immediate to the vastness of uncomprehending world of ideas and images; "Like old roses on a breeze. It would lurk for ever in ordinary things. In coat-hangers. Tomatoes. In the tar on the roads. In certain colours. In the plates at a restaurant. In the absence of words. And the emptiness in eyes" (p. 55).

One of the key elements of art is the artist's unique vision. All movements, manifestations, artistic quirks, peripheral categories and techniques must contribute to the vision. Roy's vision expressed through this novel is blurred. The novel has no profound message to offer. It seems to be the result of the author's hatred and malice towards some people. Negative emotions do not last; only virtues endure. Communism based on class war and hatred for the bourgeois is giving ground while Christianity rooted in love and goodwill is gaining ground.

Interestingly, Roy is not making any toll claims. In an interview she remarked : "My book is not the best book...It is the luckier book" (p. viii, Rao, *The Hindu Magazine*, Nov. 23). "Yes, indeed, it is "the luckier book, fetching her three crore rupees as advance, and a little more, from the Rs. five crore sales. Her novel is the most materialistic novel written in this century and will remain as the most popular novel of this decade. Roy has taken special care to cater for the demands of the modern public. There is 'sex' in chapter 21, 'violence' in chapter 19, a Joycean (James Joyce and Marquez and Roy's favourites) touch of language to make contextual sense, and sustained humour,... What else does a modern reader demand?

A classic is a star radiating its brillance through ages and ages to come; *The God of Small Things* is a flash of lightning which shocks and astonishes the reader for a moment, and for a moment only.

REFERENCES

Rao, Ranga, "The Book (er) of the Year," *The Hindu Magazine Literary Review* (November 16, 1997) : 4, xiii.

——. "The Book (er) of the year" *The Hindu Magazine* (November 23, 1997) : ii, viii.

Roy, Arundhati. *The God of Small Things,* New Delhi : India Ink, 1997.

Rushdie, Salman. *Midnight's Children.* 1980, New York : Avon Books, 1982.

——. *The Satanic Verses.* 1998, The USA : The Consortium Inc, 1992.

17

Dalit in "The God of Small Things"

—*M.B. Gaijan*

सर्वेऽत्र सुखिनः सर्वे सन्तु निरामयाः।
सर्वे भद्रानि पश्यन्तु मा कश्चित् दुःखमाप्नुयात्।।

"HERE, all should become happy, all should emancipate from the anxiety and agony, all should see the prosperity and progress of others, none should suffer any pain."

This was not truth for every Indian in the past but for the upper varnas. Because since the Vedic era, the Hindu Society was/is divided into the graded in equality and hierarchical anarchy. "वसुदैव कुटुम्बकम् Vasudaiva Kutyumbakam" was only an utopia. Because of the graded in equality, the one section of Hindu society was always remained exploited and neglected, and even that was not considered as touchable creature. This community was disgustingly separated as untouchable. Thus the untouchability is a centuries old, deeply rooted Hindu's inhuman belief. According to the superstition, "a touchable would defile, if he would touch an untouchable." It was injustice, practised by the Hindu society since long. The touchable, since past to the present time have not accepted untouchables as fellow human beings. Though the Hindu spirituality depicted in the Vedas, The Upanishads, the Purans and the Smritees emphasized on "Human Equality, Enlightenment, Uplift, Love and Kindness" to all, not only to human beings but also for every living creature. But generally this spirituality remained untouchable by the Hindu society. In these works simultaneously it is also depicted that one community was always oppressed. That was none but Dasa, Dasyu, Shudra, Untouchables, later an

Harijan and again Dalit. Mahatma Gandhi had painfully said about the social evil as "a disgrace on Hinduism" (Gandhi, M.K.).

Gandhi's idea to uplift untouchable by changing Hindu's hearts was never materialized. Thanks to the British Empire, during their rule; they first time legally tried to remove the social evil by imposing various laws. They were "The Widow Remarriage Act of 1876" and "The Caste Disability Removal Act of 1850." After the independence various constitutional rights are provided to uplift the oppressed community. Amendments after amendments are introduced but the centuries old disgust towards untouchables is not yet changed. That disgust has taken the new shape, like the old wine in the new bottle.

In the democratic India, at the end of the 20th century, still the untouchability is existing this truth. Arundhati has brought before the world. "The God of Small Things," the prestigious 'Booker Prize' awarded novel, depicts the cross caste conflict. As a matter of fact, caste and sub-caste based social divisions we find in the Hindu Society since long. Untouchables are only found in the Hindu religious works, not in Islam or in Christianity. Christianity is world-wide known for universal "brotherhood and humanism" but here, in this novel Arundhati has described the intense cross caste conflict, the conflict is not taking place between touchable Hindus and Untouchables, its between Syrian Christians and Untouchable! It shows that untouchables are not only suffering torturing and harassment from Hindus but also from other religious communities in this democratic India. Thus untouchables are sandwiched between the Hindu majority and other religious minority.

In this novel, Ayemenem, a small village in Kerala is very significant place. Ammu, a young woman whose father had worked as joint director in Imperial Etymology, Delhi, is very important person in the work. Being an orthodox, her father had not paid more attention on her education and selecting a suitable life partner for her. In the village like Ayemenem and the girl like Ammu has nothing to do except the household works and the waiting for the unknown bridegroom.

Nobody from her family was thinking about her wedding. Ultimately she made her own way by selecting a Bengali, working as an assistant manager in a tea estate in Assam. It was her first attempt to break the social barrier — an inter-community Love Marriage. In Rural India, even today, inter-community love marriage is not accepted. It is considered as a disgrace on family and lineage. So immediately after her marriage, she was badly treated by her own family. Unfortunately she could not enjoy her marriage life for a long time. She had realized "marriage wrong man." (38) It was too late. She had to return to her village Ayemenem with her twins Estha — a boy and Rahel — a daughter. In rural India, a divorce woman has only place to get shelter is her parents' house. In Ayemenem, she was of no where, because the orthodox old Lady Baby Kochamma, the grandmother of the twins, hatefully says "A divorced daughter had no position anywhere at all" (45). As for divorced daughter from the inter-community love marriage, she remained silent.

In Kerala, the paravans are considered as untouchables. When nobody from her family took care for her and her twins, naturally she would fascinated towards that who will love her and her kids, that was Velutha, an untouchable Dalit. Velutha taught the twins, boating and fishing. The kids enjoyed their learning because they didn't know "what was untouchability." Ammu also observed "the high delight" (175) on kids face, what else the rejected mother would expect than the happiness of her kids? The friendly meetings of the twins and Velutha had brought nearer to each other, the twins, Velutha and Ammu.

And consequently, gradually the young Ammu was fascinated towards the untouchable. She was attracted towards his exercised body "A swimmer's body. A swimmer carpenter's body" (175). Thus the sprouting of love in Ammu's bosom was very natural. The untouchable felt the same passion. Both of them have forgotten the ban "who should be loved, And how. And how much" (17). The Indian society, particularly Hindu orthodox, had imposed certain laws "Whom to Love." When we glance in the ancient literature of India, there are plenty evidences of that. According to the ban the untouchables were/are not allowed to love or marry upper caste women, while the other Varna's allowed to defile/ rape the untouchable women. Actually the inter-caste relationship was thus banned in the Matsya Puran, one of the old Puranas.

> "If a low caste man wants to marry a high caste girl, and does so, would be punished with death. Similarly a high caste women marrying a low caste man, should be punished with death."
>
> (CCXXVI, 131, II).

Though the ban preached in past but even today practised strictly in rural India. The deeply rooted hate for untouchable is still practised. It is only for the orthodox Hindu religion community but other religious communities also accept it. The rest of other religious Minority practises the Hindu social code of untouchability only to flatter the Hindu majority. But Ammu and Velutha, both had overthrown the imposed law. Here lust kindled from the both sides, no one had trapped any one. And "her seven years oblivion lifted off" (337). An untouchable's affair with a touchable woman is not granted in rural India, in any community. Even untouchables wouldn't dare to do such things because they know the consequences. Velutha's father knew the consequences, so he rushed to inform about his son's affair, with view to punish him but the lady of the house spat on his face.

Baby Kochamma, in her youth, who was fascinated towards father Mullingan, a handsome Irish Monk, has cunningly rejected the affair by saying thus :

> "How could she stand by the smells, haven't you noticed, they have a particular smell? These paravans?" (78).

She had mainly opposed the affair because it was with an untouchable. Untouchability is not depicted anywhere in the Holy books, but to flatter and please the Hindu Society, the Christian, too practised/cherish the notion. This incident was enough for the old Lady Baby Kochamma to remove an untouchable forever. It was due to the deeply rooted disgust towards touchable.

Co-incident, Sophie's death, she had selected to destory Velutha. Actually she knew the fact; Velutha was not responsible for Sophie's death but the violent flow of a river Meenachal. But because of hate and revenge, she had filed F.I.R. against an innocent untouchable. Sophie was Ammu's brother Chacko's daughter who came to India with her English mother from England. Thus, baby

Kochamma's conspiracy to remove untouchable was·due to her hatred towards Velutha.

Whenever an untouchable is accused for any crime, the touchable became united to remove him forever, it is the countrywide truth that revealed in the novel. After filing the F.I.R. against the untouchable, Velutha, at Kottayam police station. "A posse of touchable policemen crossed the Meenachal River" (304). To find out him, When they found him, at that time he was sleeping. They treated him thus inhumanly. "They wake Velutha with their boots" (307). That shows they didn't touch Velutha directly but by their boots. These were the public servants of democratic India.

When the touchable police's operation was going on, at that time the twins — Estha and Rahel — were near by Velutha. They witnessed the barbaric incident thus :

> "They realized that man was beaten, was Velutha. They heard the thud on wood on flesh. Boot on bone. On teeth the muffled grunt when a stomach is kicked in. The muted crunch of skull on cement. The gurgle of blood on a man's breath when his long is turn by the jagged end of a broken rib" (308).

Still the crime was not proved, it was only the charge, but the touchable police had brutally treated the accused untouchable as a murderer. The policemen are not given this sort of liberty to treat the accused, but it was untouchable, so granted. This sort of victimized untouchable how long he would live? "Half an hour past midnight death come for him" (320). In this cross caste love affair, Ammu was not entrapped by Velutha. Willingly she had submitted herself, but Hindu dominated Indian Society would not allow the affair. Both of them had paid the highest price for that. Velutha was killed and Ammu's family was scattered.

The climax of Ammu's misery was the Christian Inspector Thomas Mathew's malicious behavior. When she reached at the Kottayam Police Station to inform the truth about Sophie's death and save Velutha, nobody has noticed her. But the police inspector Mathew, by tapping on her breasts with his baton, said, "The Kottayam police station did not take statements from Vaishayas or illegitimate children" (8). What was her crime? love? Actually she had thrown away the imposed social code of Hindu's. Whom to Love, but not the Christian code. She had not done anything wrong but loved an untouchable, and consequently she became an untouchable vaishya whose breasts can be touched. Touched by baton! It shows that the Christian minority in India also tries to flatter and please the Hindu majority by hating the Untouchables.

The hatred towards untouchables cannot be removed until the society would accept them as the fellow human beings. By giving special rights or political protection that may be erased. In Kerala, the communists were in power; still it is the powerful political party. They have accepted human Liberty, Equality and Fraternity. But in the case of untouchables, they change the policy. Velutha was a card holder party member. When the Christian family knew his love affair, consequently he felt his life was in danger, he immediately rushed to the party leader, Mr. Pillai, to interfere the issue. But Mr. Pillai had shrewdly rejected his request thus "party was not constituted to support workers indiscipline in their private life" (287). If he would interfere in the case, Velutha wouldn't die thus. Mr. Pillai had refused to help Velutha on the base of "indiscipline in their private life" but the truth was something else. The communists were not out of the caste based social clutch :

> "The Marxist worked from within the communal divides, never challenging them, never appearing not to" (66, 67).

Thus the novelist has portrayed the socio-political realism of democratic India, where still one community is becoming the victim of the brutality of the majority and the flatterers of the majority. "The God of Small Things" is a story about love and brutality (B. Urvashi), the brutality against the Dalits. On one hand, the Human Rights and values are globally, seriously considered, on other hand, in rural India, this sort of atrocity against Dalits are going on. The Aymenem incident of killing Velutha is the microscopic vision of the orthodoxy's brutality against Dalits. In India, plenty legal protections are provided to remove the atrocity against Dalits but they are only on the papers.

It wouldn't change until the social attitude would change. If the Indian society would accept them, they wouldn't remain untouchable, socially and culturally. They would merge with the main stream. Then More Veluthas wouldn't die.

REFERENCES

1. Butalia Urvashi, "Blessed Are They Who Read This," *The Book Rev.* Vol. XXI, No. 5, May 97, pp. 28.
2. John Binook, "The New Deity of Prose," *India Today*, Oct 27, 97, pp. 26.
3. Gandhi M.K., "Varna Vyavastha" Ahmedabad, Navjeevan, Savant 1990, pp. 65.
4. Prarthana Preeti, Mumbai, Sat Vichar Darshan Trust 1991, pp. 16.
5. Roy Arundhati, "The God of Small Things," New Delhi India Ink, 1997.
6. The Matsya Purana.

18

Taslima Nasrin's *Lazza* : A Revolt Against Religious Persecution

—Amar Nath Prasad

> "... Our accounts of God are likely stories, but all the same legendary. Not one of them is full and final. We are like little children on the sea-shore trying to fill our shells with water from the sea. While we cann't exhaust the waters of the deep by means of our shells, every drop that we attempt to gather into our tiny shells is a part of authentic waters."[1]
>
> *—S. Radhakrishnan*

TASLIMA Nasrin, a universal best-seller novelist, shot into literary limelight after her controversial book, "Lazza." In theme, the novel truthfully portrays the horrendous and horrifying experience of a minority family, the Duttas-Sudhamoy, Kironmoyee and their two children — Suranjan and Maya, who have to face so many trials and tribulations, insult and abuse without any rhyme or reason — just only because of their Hindu identity in Bangladesh; just only because Sudhamoy, an atheist believes, 'with a naive mix of optimism and idealism that his mother land will not let him down,'[2] just only because they don't want to evacuate that country they loved so much; just only because they have an ardent desire to show respect and sympathy to all religions. In tone and temper, the author seeks not a nostalgia for the golden past or rosy future, but the burning topic of day-to-day reality of religious extremism of Bangladesh were confrontation arose between Hindu and Muslim after 6 December 1992, the date Babri Masjid, the abode of God, was demolished mercilessly by a number of Hindu fundamentalists. The jacket cover of the book, "Lazza" rightly observes :

"Unremittingly dark and menacing, the novel exposes the mindless blood thirstiness of fundamentalism and brilliantly captures the insanity of violence in our time."[3]

"Lazza" is a religious satire on the bigotism and extremism of religion. But here the satire is not mild and indirect like that of "Macflecknoe" in which Dryden changed the rough to refined, the vulgar to aesthetic, and a low to sublime; the satire here is rather very harsh, poignant and denigrating like that of Alexander Pope who used decisive and abusive language to expose the hollowness of Dr. Arbuthnot.

Well, the topic of religious satire is not a new one. It was a history right from Langland to Modern age. It is, indeed, a matter of great surprise that almost every satirist of English literature had to face the religious confrontation of his contemporary age. The first great satirist in English literature is William Langland who, in his famous book, "Piers the Plowman" flings a harsh satire on the snobbery and hypocrisy of religious fundamentalism of his age. His satirical lash whips the clergy of all orders — bishops, archdeacons, monks, friars, pardoners, parish priests etc. Bishops are criticised harshly for indiscriminately giving their seals to unscrupulous persons who use them for exploiting the poor ignorant people. Friars are also vehemently lashed out. To Langland they all personify every evil on earth and are foes to every virtue. The poet observes :

> "Heremites on an heep with hoked stages,
> Wenten to Walsyngham and here wenches after;
> Grete lobyes and longe that both were to swynke,
> Clotheden hem in copies to ben known from othere
> And shopen hem heremites here ese to have."[4]

The other great satirist who flings his vent on the corruptions of religion, was Chaucer. The portraits of "The prologue to the Canterbury Tales" are satirical in nature. The poet draws of the fat, pleasure loving monk, the merry and wanton friar, the hypocrite and dull pardoner who wanders about selling indulgences and relics etc. This shows that Chaucer was alive to the shocking corruptions prevalent in religion of his time.

Milton, the great poet of English literature, also notices the drawbacks of religious ceremonies performed in the churches of his time. He exposed the dark aspects of religious spirit in his famous work, "Lycidas." He said that corrupt clergy had managed to enter the church in a stealthy and underhand way only for mere material consideration. They make little account of any other duty than how to struggle for church endowments. They have absolutely no idea of their religious duties and their gospel :

> "Blind Mouths! that scarce themselves to know how to hold
> A sheep-hook, or have learned aught else the least
> That to the faithful herdman's art belongs!
> What reeks it them? What need they? They are sped."[5]

Religious extremism can also be found in the age of Dryden and Pope. In "The Hind and the Panther, a Defence of the Roman Church," Dryden boldly exposes the corruptions and abberrations of the Church. But this work didn't receive any pecuniary gain from its publication. To quote Arthur Compton-Rickett : "The following year, when William and Mary came to the throne, and Protestantism was in the ascendant, Dryden fell on evil days; the pensions accompanying his public appointments were withdrawn, and worst of all he had the chagrin of seeing Shadwell appointed to the Laureateship that had been his for eighteen years."[6] This statement clearly shows that religious exposure is such a sensitive activity that it is bound to be punished. It is not simply the case of Bangladesh where a number of Muslim Fundamentalist rose against Taslima Nasrin; or the case of India where a handful of Hindu religious extremists are dead against the arrival of Pope in India; or the case of Iran where a 'fatwa' was imposed on Salman Rushdie who wrote a controversial book, "The Satanic Verses;" but it is a case in almost every nook and corner of the world.

Well, like Taslima Nasrin, Jonathan Swift also satirized the hateful fanaticism and shameful bigotism of his time in a ludicrous manner. His book, "A Tale of a Tub" symbolically satirizes the pride and fanaticism of the contemporary society. A considerable portion of this great work is occupied by an account of the quarrels of the churches. It deals with the story of the three brothers — Peter, Martin and Jack who represent the Roman Catholics, the Anglicans and the Puritans respectively. Even T.S. Eliot, in modern time, has shown the loss of faith and sterility of religion in his famous poem, "Gerontion." He says that under the influence of science and rationalism, there is outright rejection of faith on the part of the many. There are also some people who accept God and His teachings mechanically without any passional participation. Such acceptance, according to T.S. Eliot, is mere empty ritual-availing nothing :

> "In depraved May, dogwood and chestnut, flowering judas:
> To be eaten, to be divided, to be drunk—
> Among whispers."[7]

Thus, this brief survey of religious satire clearly shows that religion is the most senstitive part of human life and so it should be handled carefully. Now the question is : Why is it that the people of Bangladesh (specially those people who are mad with fanaticism) went berserk against the truthful portrayal of Taslima Nasrin — an author who dares to expose the evils of her own religion? Is it essential on the part of the 'guardians of religion' (Mullah, Pandit and Priests) to give orders to shoot the author, the torch-bearer of a nation? Is it not wrong to ban a book which gives you light — which makes you aware of your shortcomings? Certainly, it is the most shameful act on the part of a nation to lock the mouth of free thought. An author is the voice of a nation. He can herald an upheaval in the realm of traditional or conservative thinking. If he stops unfurling corruptions and abberations of a nation, then, who will do this job? Businessman? Politicians? Doctors? Lawyers? Oh! No! This duty goes only to the thinkers and authors, poets and philosophers. Shakespeare rightly observes :

> "The poet's eye, in a fine frenzy rolling,
> Doth glance from heaven to earth, from earth to heaven.
> And as imagination bodies forth
> The forms of things unknown, the poet's pen
> Turns them to shapes, and gives to airy nothing
> A local habitation and a name."[8]

The book, "Lazza" opens with the restlessness of a frightened Hindu family in Bangladesh after the shameful abolition of a Great Masjid, called Babri Masjid in Ayodhaya. Maya, the sister of Suranjan, the protoganist of the novel, is very fearful and wants to flee away from the country. But Suranjan, on the other hand, was in a rebellious mood. He fumes and mutters like an angry tiger : "Why should he flee his home simply because his name was Suranjan Dutta? Was it necessary for his family — Sudhamoy, his father, Kironmoyee, his mother and Nilanjana (Maya), his sister — to run away like fugitives just because of their names? Would they have to take refuge in the homes of Kamal, Belal or Haider just as they had done two years back? ... Why did he have to run away from his, own home? And wasn't this country as much his as it was Kamal's? Then why was he seemingly deprived of his rights; and why was his motherland turning her back on him?"

Sudhamoy, the father of Suranjan, recollects some past events in a stream of consciousness method. He remembers how in 1947, all his aunts and uncles and other relatives had begun to leave Bangladesh one by one; how in 1952, the people of this country specially, the young, brave and politically conscious Bengalis of East Pakistan rose in protest against Urdu language imposed by Jinnah; how in 1969, Pakistani Strongman, Ayub Khan, passed standing instruction to fire at processions; how in 1971, he witnessed wave upon wave of bloodshed and trouble.

It is to be noted here that Suranjan, though a Hindu, possesses only a little sense of Hinduism in his heart. He is a man who believes that all religions, however, different they may be, are one and the same. He has no grudge against any Muslim friend. But the irony lies in it, that in spite of his neutral and secular nature, he had to face so many untold miseries, abuse and taunts. According to the novelist, he was a man who believed that no religion had created barriers. He wanted to see his people away from communal barriers and live together in perfect harmony. Moreover, he was also a staunch patriot who preferred dying in the soil of his country to take shelter in India. But in spite of all these things, his family has to be enmeshed in the net of bigotry and communalism. Suranjan thought why people tried to avoid him and excluded him from their groups. He felt like a fish out of water. He thought that 'only human beings had racial and communal differences and only they had temples and mosques' (p. 59). He also meditated that cats have no communal differences. She goes to the kitchen, of both Hindu and Muslim alike :

"Suranjan attention was drawn to the animal. Hadn't the cat been to the Dhakeshwari temple today? Which community did the cat belong to? Was it Hindu? Presumably it was Hindu, since it lived in a Hindu home. It was a black and white cat and there was a softness about its eyes. It seemed to pity him. If it had the ability to pity, the cat must be Muslim! Must be a liberal Muslim! ... The cat got up and left. Perhaps it was going to the Muslim kitchen next door, since there wasn't much food being cooked in this house" (p. 59).

Well, religion is the part and parcel of man's life. A race without religion is just like a flower without fragrance, a body without heart. There have been degraded religions as well as lofty religions producing evil as well as good. But so far as man's journey to peace and prosperity, purity and spirituality is concerned, religion has accompanied man at every stage of time. In short, religion is an organising idea and it is the cohesive force in man's social structure. It is the greatest and most immediate need of human being. Mahatma Gandhi rightly holds the view :

"No man can live without religion. There are some who in the egotism of their reason declare that they have nothing to do with religion. But it is like a man saying that he breathes but that he has no nose. Whether by reason or by instinct or by superstition, man acknowledges some sort of relationship with the divine. The rankest agnostic or atheist does acknowledge the need of a moral principle and associates something good with its observance and something bad with the non-observance."[9]

But the greatest irony lies in it that in spite of the perennial significance of religion, most of the fanatics of the world don't understand the real purport of religious spirit; they begin to hurl insult and abuse on other's religion. As a matter of fact, all religions of the world, however, different in form they may be, are essentially the same. Though their creeds, practices, rituals, customs and rites, differ immensely from one another, yet if one dives deep into the soul of it, one finds a cohesive and universal unity among them. So, if a Hindu tortures a Muslim on the ground of religion, it is his greatest foolishness and *vice-versa*. We should always bear in our mind that all religions project and express the same Eternal Truth — God is one; He is our Father or Mother or Friend. Or He is Omnipotent, Omnicient and Omnipresent. Or in the tent of God, all creatures are equal. In short, all religions of the universe are the small rivers and rivulets which are flowing to die deep into the bosom of the Almighty Sea. S. Radhakrishnan has rightly quoted the observation of Bohme in his famous book, "The Hindu View of Life" :

"Consider the birds in our forests, they praise God each in his own way, in diverse tones and fashions. Think you God is vexed by this diversity and desires to silence discordant voices? All the forms of being are dear to the infinite Being Himself."[10] Moreover, Kabirdas was also dead against the hypocricy and artificiality of rituals. He lashed out the Hindu who used to worship the stone blindly without caring for his own inner purification. On the other hand, he also exposed the hypocricy of those Mullah who practised just the otherwise of what they taught. So no religion is good and no religion is bad. All religions are perfect in their own jurisdiction. Any attempt to falsify or disparage other religious belief will surely lead to fanaticism which cann't be called good at any cost. What is needed today is not to degrade the belief of the other but to peep into the inner chamber of oneself and to eradicate the plants of fanaticism if it is gaining ground. Religious extremism in any form mustn't be tolerated at any cost. Why? Because it is just like a poisonous insect which eats into the vitals of a healthy religion or it is a disease of the rose which slowly but steadily rots the beauty of the flower. So both the Hindu and the Muslim should never develop a sense of hatred and jealousy to each other. Rather they should try their best to admire and appreciate their different beliefs though they are not different at all in the depth. To quote S. Radhakrishnan again : "People may come from different directions, approach different ways so long as they are pilgrims on the road they may have their differences, they may have their quarrels, but when the pilgrims reach that end of their quest, they will feel that they belong to one supreme family, they form kindred spirits, whether they come from Islam, Christianity, Hinduism or Buddhism, they all belong to the Church of Christ, or Buddha or Muhammad... but we all do belong to the church of One Universal Spirit, which is called by different names in different religions."[11]

Thus, this brief survey clearly shows that the callous and inhuman treatment shouldn't be done on the basis of religion. It is time that "the darkness be dissipated and the clouds of misunderstanding dispersed, and the light must shine in all the activities which we perform."[12] So, both the Hindu and the Muslim mustn't forget that all people are the children of the Supreme God and therefore there cann't be any real distinction between one race and another, or one nation or another. To quote again Radhakrishnan, "There is no master, race, there is no master nation, there is no master class. We are all equally citizens of this world and the children of the Supreme."[13]

The novel ends with the stumbling of Sudhamoy's strong belief in patriotism. He, more than once, said in this novel that he wouldn't leave that land at any cost. But now, he is so much threatened by the fundamentalists of his beloved motherland that he is ready to go to 'India' the country where "live and let live" is the main motto of the general people; where the voice of the country is to give proper respect for all other creeds (though a bit impaired during the abolition of the Great Mosque in Ayodhya). The author takes the image of a whirlpool which swept the protagonist into the depths : "He was caught in a whirlpool and kept sinking gradually. He wanted to live, but there was no one to pull him to the shore. As he kept sinking into the fathomless waters, Suranjan found he was sweating." Through this beautiful and appropriate image, the author means to say that religious fundamentalism is a whirlpool which lacks the qualm of conscience and swallows away everything — good or bad; vulgar or refine; low or sublime. So, the main motto of Taslima Nasrin is to protest persecution and discrimination. In the preface of the book, she holds the view : "The disease of religious fundamentalism is not restricted to Bangladesh alone and it must be fought at every turn. For myself, I am not afraid of any challenge or threat to my life. I will continue to write and protest persecution and discrimination.

I am convinced that the only way the fundamentalist forces can be stopped is if all of us who are secular and humanistic join together and fight their malignant influence. I, for one, will not be silenced."[14]

Thus, "Lazza" by Taslima Nasrin deals with a universal problem of fanaticism. This problem is so cancerous that if it is not treated timely, it will kill the healthy values of religion. It is time we should pay a heed to the invocation of Katha Upanisad :

> "May (Brahman) equally protect us;
> May we equally share the benefit of the knowledge;
> May we both be equally strong to receive the knowledge;
> May our learning be equally fruitful;
> May we n't be jealous of each other.
> Peace (for oneself), peace (for the environment),
> peace (for the animal world)."[15]

REFERENCES

1. Dr. S. Radhakrishnan, *The Hindu View of Life* (Unwin Books, London, 1963), p. 27.
2. Jacket Cover, "Lazza" by Taslima Nasrin, (Penguin Books Nehru Place, New Delhi, 1993), subsequent references are to this edition.
3. *Ibid.*
4. William Langland, "Piers the Plowman" (Lakshmi Narain Agarwal Educational Pub., Agra), p. 58.
5. Milton, *Lycidas* edited by N.M. Kulkarni (Lakshmi Narain Agarwal Educational Pub., Agra), p. 58.
6. Arthur Compton-Rickett, *A History of English Literature* (Thomas Nelson and Sons Ltd., London, 1955), p. 197.
7. T.S. Eliot, "Gerontion", *The Golden Treasury* edited by F.T. Palgrave (Oxford University Press, Delhi, 1988), p. 474.
8. Shakespeare, *The Lunatic, the Lover, and the Poet, A Many Coloured Glass*, edited by D.D. Baskiyar (Orient Longman, Ltd., Calcutta, 1987), p. 3.
9. Mahatma Gandhi, *The Need for Religion, Intermediate English Prose Selection*, edited by K.C. Srivastava (Oxford University Press, New Delhi, 1977), p. 24.
10. Dr. S. Radhakrishnan, *The Hindu View of Life* (Unwin Books, Lond., 1963), p. 27.
11. Dr. S. Radhakrishnan, *The Inward Light, Perspectives on Modern English Prose*, edited by K.S. Ramamurti (Vikas Publishing House Pvt. Ltd., Delhi, 1990), p. 16.

12. *Ibid.*, p. 19.
13. *Ibid.*, p. 17.
14. Taslima Nasrin, "Lazza", Preface (Penguin Books, New Delhi, 1993).
15. Katha Upanishad, Translated by Swami Lokeshwarananda (The Ram Krishna Mission Institute of Culture, Gol Park, Calcutta, 1993), p. 5.